"*Into the Mirror* by Andy F
that help deconstruct ma
vade modernity. Andy has an engaging and provocative writing
style, making our path to a deeper understanding stimulating and
potentially transformative."

—Tsoknyi Rinpoche, coauthor of *Why We Meditate*

"Andy Karr's *Into the Mirror* is a brilliant companion volume
to his *Contemplating Reality*. In the mirror of our mind, all kinds
of inner and outer phenomena appear like reflections, but
when we really look deeply into that mirror, all we see is our own
true face. Whether this is called 'pure awareness,' 'buddha nature,'
or 'awakening,' it is the basic ground of our experience. If not recognized, it is delusion; if recognized, it is primordial wakefulness
full of wisdom and compassion. This book is a significant and very
accessible contribution to the ongoing dialogue between 'modern'
philosophy, psychology, and cognitive science and the 'ancient'
Buddhist inner science of introspection and contemplation."

—Karl Brunnhölzl, author of *Luminous Heart*

"It is rare to find a book on Buddhist wisdom teachings that shows
us how actually to put them into practice, so it is delightful to see
how Karr walks the reader through these teachings step by step,
with clarity and humor. Karr warmly invites us into this stream of
wisdom and encourages us to jump in."

—Judith Lief, author of *Making Friends with Death*

"With no lab other than meditation, Buddhist philosophers have
developed sophisticated theories of mind and reality. Andy Karr
presents a lucid survey of this tradition and holds it next to
modern theories of consciousness. From that conversation arise
beautifully subversive questions like whether the point is not the
relationship between immaterial mind and material brain but how
they might both be manifestations of something else, and conun-
drums like how you can have subjective experience without a self.
A thoughtful and thought-provoking book."

—Joan Sutherland, author of *Through Forests of Every Color*

"There are two common assumptions about consciousness in modern thinking: that the mind can be reduced to something material and non-experiential and that it is forever destined to remain a mystery. Both these assumptions distance us from actually exploring the nature of knowing. Karr exposes the frailty and blind spots of scientific materialism and guides us toward ancient Buddhist methods of exploring mind through 'first-person science.' A thoughtful, engaging, and timely book."

—Elizabeth Mattis Namgyel, author of *The Logic of Faith*

"Andy Karr invites us to consider the materialistic benefits of modern times. Have they made us happy? And if not, what then? This is a key issue for our time, and *Into the Mirror* adroitly lays out traditional and contemporary insights on how we might tame the materialistic matrix. His orientation is blessedly complete—starting with skillful insights into foundations of Buddhist thought and then questioning contemporary framings of consciousness as a problem to solve. These catalyze appreciation for a profound journey toward resolving what most fundamentally ails us. Eminently readable. Eminently nourishing."

—Anne Carolyn Klein, author of *Heart Essence of the Vast Expanse*

INTO
THE
MIRROR

A Buddhist Journey through Mind,
Matter, and the Nature of Reality

ANDY KARR

FOREWORD BY MATTHIEU RICARD

SHAMBHALA

Shambhala Publications, Inc.
2129 13th Street
Boulder, Colorado 80302
www.shambhala.com

Cover photo: Andy Karr
Cover design: Daniel Urban-Brown
Interior design: Katrina Noble

9 8 7 6 5 4 3 2 1

First Edition
Printed in the United States of America

Shambhala Publications makes every effort to print on acid-free, recycled paper.
Shambhala Publications is distributed worldwide by Penguin Random House, Inc.,
and its subsidiaries.

LIBRARY OF CONGRESS CATALOGING-IN-PUBLICATION DATA
Names: Karr, Andy, author.
Title: Into the mirror: a Buddhist journey through mind, matter, and the nature of
    reality / Andy Karr.
Description: Boulder: Shambhala, 2023. | Includes bibliographical references.
Identifiers: LCCN 2022023188 | ISBN 9781645471646 (trade paperback)
Subjects: LCSH: Spiritual life—Buddhism. | Buddhism—Doctrines. | Buddhism and
    science.
Classification: LCC BQ4302 .K366 2023 | DDC 294.3/444—dc23/eng/20220825
LC record available at https://lccn.loc.gov/2022023188

Although I dwell in the slime and muck of the dark age,
I still aspire to see your face.
Although I stumble in the thick, black fog of materialism,
I still aspire to see your face.

—CHÖGYAM TRUNGPA, *The Sadhana of Mahamudra*

CONTENTS

FOREWORD

As often stressed in Buddhist scriptures, all sentient beings aspire to happiness but often turn their back to it. They all dread suffering, but they often run toward the sharp blade of the law of cause and effect that brings them torments of all kinds. No one wakes up in the morning thinking "May I suffer the whole day and, if possible, my whole life." Yet because of ignorance and delusion, we seem to be addicted to the causes of suffering. As my root teacher Dilgo Khyentse Rinpoche said, "To expect happiness without giving up negative action is like holding your hand in a fire and hoping not to be burned."[1]

As Andy Karr shows eloquently in *Into the Mirror*, one of the main characteristics of ignorance is to adopt a materialistic perspective about life, consciousness, and the world at large. Revealing the flaws of a materialistic worldview is not a rejection of the world, as it leads to fully embracing limitless beings with limitless compassion, thus fulfilling the Bodhisattva's ideal.

As Karr points out, this does not mean making concessions to the endless demands and mystifications of our ego, particularly in relation to the eight worldly concerns—gain and loss, pleasure and pain, praise and blame, fame and shame. Such concerns bring nothing but frustration to oneself and others. To remedy this state of affairs, we need to have the willingness and courage to open our minds to the teachings of the enlightened ones, from the Buddha to the present holders of authentic lineages conveying ageless wisdom.

Into the Mirror stresses the crucial importance of being in accord with reality, in other words of ceasing to superimpose our mental fabrications on the way things are. We take that which changes at every moment as permanent and believe in the existence of separate entities endowed with intrinsic properties, while the phenomenal world is in flux and interdependent events are devoid of inherent and autonomous existence. This is not just some arcane philosophical matter, as it deals with the very root of suffering. In short, one of the fundamental aims of Buddhist philosophy and practice is to bridge the gap between appearances and reality.

A significant part of this book focuses on examining materialistic and reductionist views on consciousness. In so doing, Karr shows that none of these various approaches—eliminativist, physicalist, mysterion, etc.—can satisfactorily account for the fact that consciousness is primarily an experience.

In essence, there are two main ways of approaching consciousness: from the outside (the third-person perspective) or from the inside (the first-person perspective). The third-person perspective corresponds to the study of the correlates of conscious phenomena in the brain, the nervous system, and our behavior as it can be observed by a third person. The first-person perspective is the actual experience of the mind knowing the mind.

Even if the gigantic endeavor to map the three hundred billion neurons of the brain would succeed and one could describe in every possible detail what happens in the brain when someone sees the color red or feels love or hate, the precise description of what neurons do would not give us the slightest clue about what it is to experience seeing red, feeling love, or tasting wild honey without experiencing these directly. Without such a direct experience, one cannot speak of consciousness at all, and there is no way to step out of consciousness to study it, the brain, or anything else.

As my dear colleague philosopher Michel Bitbol wrote, "The creators of objective knowledge become so impressed by its efficacy that they tend to forget or to minimize that conscious experience is its starting point and its permanent requirement."[2] This is known as the "hard problem" faced by those who want to explain consciousness in purely reductionist ways as something entirely describable in terms of a complex organization of matter. (The "easy problem," which is already difficult enough, but may eventually be solved, is to know perfectly the functioning of the brain down to the most minute detail.)

In a dialogue I had a few years ago with the philosopher Daniel Dennett, a preeminent representative of one of the most extreme versions of materialism, *eliminativism*, he bluntly summarized his view: "There is no hard problem about consciousness, because consciousness does not exist." He hoped in this way to get rid of the "hard problem." But how could something that does not exist probe its own existence or nonexistence?

At the beginning of *Consciousness: Confessions of a Romantic Reductionist*, Christof Koch writes, "Without consciousness, there is nothing."[3] It is nice to hear such a statement from a very smart reductionist. In fact, without consciousness, we couldn't even claim that the world exists because that statement already implies the presence of a consciousness.

When I'm looking into my mind with my mind, I notice some thoughts, some perceptions of the outer world and inner reactions to these perceptions; I recall memories, go through emotions and reasoning; I feel attraction and repulsion, joys and sorrows, and so on. Behind all these movements of thoughts, there is a basic faculty of knowing. If I go deeper and deeper into it, I reach nothing else but pure awareness, the most fundamental state of experience, which is like reaching quarks or the quantum vacuum when investigating the fundamental aspect of matter. If I then apply Leibniz's question to consciousness—"Why is there consciousness rather than nothing?"—all I can do is acknowledge the presence of pure experience. Hence, we can say that consciousness is a primary fact.[4]

Buddhism's conception is radically different from Cartesian dualism, which postulates, on one side, a truly existing solid material reality and, on the other side, a completely immaterial consciousness that cannot have any real connection with matter. The Buddhist analysis of phenomena recognizes the lack of intrinsic reality of *all* phenomena: whether animate or inanimate, they are equally devoid of autonomous, ultimate existence. Accordingly, for Buddhism the seemingly irreconcilable duality between the material world and an immaterial consciousness, is a false problem, given that neither of them has an intrinsic, independent existence.

Karr does not stop there, and in the third and last part of this wonderful book, he takes us on a tour of the main tenets of Mahayana philosophy, the heart essence of Buddhist thought articulated by Nagarjuna and other great Indian panditas and further explained by major Tibetan commentators. Altogether he offers us a very engaging and enriching book that will help many readers unravel some essential points from the measureless treasury of Buddhist teachings.

MATTHIEU RICARD

PROLOGUE

Imagine:

You wake up. The day begins. Even before you open your eyes, an image of some guy from work arises in your mind. You lay in bed, fretting about having to deal with him again. How can you avoid another confrontation? You struggle with your memories of how you handled the last conflict and strategize about what you could do next time.

You open your eyes. Reluctantly, you get out of bed and head to the kitchen. While making coffee and toast, you go through your list of worriables for the day. There are lots of things on your desk, and you've also got some large bills coming due. That leads you to thinking about money, your meager savings, and the things that could go wrong in your life that would open a black hole in your savings account: you could get sick, have an accident, get too old to work . . .

As you eat your breakfast, you look at the news on your phone, and another headline about some dreadful politician pops up. You devour the latest conflicts and disasters along with your toast, and your stomach churns. You feel like you are in the middle of a maelstrom. You ask yourself, How will this end?

Finishing your meal, you rush through your morning ablutions, worrying about getting to work. You dress, and as you finish, you look at yourself in the mirror, and for the umpteenth time you notice your waistline and groan.

Suddenly, you realize that you are looking at a reflection. It is not *you* in the mirror at all! The sensory world becomes quite vivid. You realize that all the images that have streamed through your mind since you woke up—your antagonist, financial burdens, tribal politics, body fat—are all just like the appearances in a dream. They are like waves that rise up out of the ocean and dissolve back into the ocean. They arise in your own mind and dissolve back into your own mind. You see that the expanse of mind is clear and open, like the sky. And you relax.

This is an illustration of two ways of seeing. The confused way takes all the images that arise in your mind as facts about reality: enticing facts or oppressive facts, promises or threats, gods or demons. The other way of seeing is to recognize these appearances for what they are: mind-stuff—mere transient mental phenomena.

You may have already glimpsed this second way of seeing. The premise of the buddhadharma is that this way of seeing reveals the truth of genuine reality, and becoming accustomed to genuine reality is the path to liberation.

Seeing the truth won't get rid of the jerk at work. It won't fix your financial problems. It won't change the results of the next election. It won't shrink your waistline. But it will liberate you from the tyranny of your own projections so that you can face whatever you experience with openness, spontaneity, and compassion.

INTRODUCTION

Dispelling the Darkness

Why did the groundbreaking Buddhist teacher Chögyam Trungpa Rinpoche declare, "This is the darkest hour of the dark ages"?[1] It's worth contemplating.

This is an age of extraordinary material progress. In the developed world, most of us enjoy life spans, comforts, and possessions that are beyond the wildest dreams of even kings and queens of former times—let alone ordinary folk. And yet, this immense bounty has its somber side. All these material advances have not been able to bring us genuine freedom or lasting happiness.

We spend our lives trying to feed a deep hunger for security, comfort, and entertainment, without ever getting to the source of our discontent. Today, consumerism is rampant. Inequality and oppression are everywhere. The accumulation of knowledge is valued more than the insight needed to use it wisely. Human exploitation of the natural world has been disastrous for many of the beings with whom we share the planet. One million species of animals and plants are now threatened with extinction.[2] The immensity of human impact on the environment has created a climate crisis that threatens our entire civilization.

Don't get me wrong. Science and technology are not enemies of our well-being. The intellectual and material achievements of science and technology are worthy of great respect. Many of these—modern medicine to name just one example—have been extremely beneficial. I cannot imagine living in a world without antibiotics, vaccines, or pasteurization.[3] Nevertheless, it's clear that the accumulation of material wealth and knowledge has not led to a corresponding increase in spiritual wealth and social harmony.

Trungpa Rinpoche diagnosed the cause of this failure:

The river of materialism has burst its banks.
The materialistic outlook dominates everywhere
And the mind is intoxicated with worldly concerns.[4]

Materialism here is the instinctive belief that fulfillment and freedom will come from possessing things. Drawing on a traditional metaphor, Trungpa Rinpoche described three versions of this instinct as "three lords of materialism": the "lord of form," "lord of speech," and "lord of mind." These lords seem to promise riches and liberation, but to our surprise, they end up enslaving us.

The lord of form seduces with physical objects: "That new phone is really cool and it will bring me joy." "That guy will be fun and a supportive friend." "That promotion will provide financial security and a chance to make my mark." "That outfit will make me look quite attractive." The joy, the support, the security, and the attractiveness seem to be real properties of the things we seek, but they are just the come-ons of the lord of form. If you manage to get what you want, the joy will invariably be fleeting.

The lord of speech seduces with intellectual knowledge: "I am learning psychology to understand how people tick." "I am studying Italian to be more sophisticated." "I want to become an artist to express my creativity." The lord of speech offers us mastery over our lives through accumulating knowledge and skills, but the promises are just as hollow as those of the lord of form. Even if you acquire the knowledge and skills that you want, you will still have to face the difficulties of life.

The lord of mind seduces with psychological and spiritual objects: "I practice yoga to enjoy relaxation and bliss." "Therapy will help me become happy." "I meditate to become peaceful." The lord of mind turns spiritual and psychological states into still more merchandise that will never live up to the marketing.

From a distance, the lords of materialism seem to offer fulfillment. When we manage to possess what they offer, sooner or later we find that the joke is on us. This disappointment only increases our hunger for more. The three lords of materialism all have a common basis: mistaking our mental projections for real things.

At a deeper level, materialism—or physicalism, as it is sometimes called—is a view about the nature of reality.[5] It is the belief that reality consists entirely of the stuff described by physics. This is an assumption that subtly pervades the entire modern world. An example is believing that mind is merely functions of the brain. Materialism reifies our sense of being embedded in a fixed, independently existing physical reality, and it dismisses the mind as nothing more than "a ghost in the machine." This dogma reinforces the power of the lords of materialism. If mind is an illusion, and all that exists is physical stuff, you might as well just get what you can.

Because materialist views are so deeply ingrained in contemporary culture and education, they are almost invisible. The darkness of materialism can only be overcome by the light of wisdom. The Mahayana path of contemplation and meditation is an inner journey that reveals this wisdom. On this path, freeing yourself goes hand in hand with helping to liberate others.

My goal in writing this book was to offer a fresh approach to the Mahayana teachings that is adapted to our contemporary conditions and worldview. To do this, I have done my best to draw on the deep insights, practices, and history of the tradition. Because the menaces we face today are shaped by specific conditions of modernity, which traditional teachings never needed to address, I have also included investigations from contemporary philosophers that challenge the intellectual foundations of materialism.

I believe that we need to engage with the tools of modernity to combat the materialist views that modernity has unleashed. The thought experiments, insights, and perspectives that these contemporary philosophers offer have helped me surface and examine my own hidden assumptions about the nature of the natural world, while at the same time deepening my appreciation for the Mahayana path. It is clear to me that unless we grapple with— and overcome—these implicit assumptions, it will be extremely difficult to realize the profundity of the buddhadharma.

This book is divided into three parts.

The first part of the book, "Starting from Square One," is an orientation for the journey. It explores themes from the Foundational Vehicle[6] and aligns them with the Mahayana view. This includes revisiting the Buddha's four truths, the notion of enlightenment, and various topics related to the practice of meditation. These are teachings that we encounter at the beginning of the Buddhist journey but whose profundity and vastness only become apparent as we study, practice, and go through life experiences. By contemplating these topics again and again as we progress along the path, our understanding will become subtler and deeper.

The second part of the book, "Overcoming Materialism," offers methods for surfacing hidden assumptions about the nature of reality and deconstructing the conceptual underpinnings of materialism. It begins by introducing what modern philosophers call "the hard problem of consciousness." This is essentially another way of posing the classical mind-body problem. To explore this problem, we examine various materialist positions and contemporary challenges to them.

This section concludes with a modest proposal for a shift in perspective on the hard problem. The dominant contemporary assumption is that matter is fundamental, and the hard problem is explaining how consciousness could arise from it. When we recognize that we can never escape the perspective of experience to establish the existence of anything extramental, dualistic assumptions about mind and matter collapse. From this new perspective, the hard problem is seen to be understanding how reality, which seems so solid, can arise from mind. This formulation provides an excellent foundation for the Mahayana journey that follows.

Once the first part of the book has oriented us toward the profound and the second part of the book has surfaced and undermined materialistic beliefs, we are ready to proceed to the third part of the book, "A Profound Journey," which takes us to the heart of the matter. This is where we explore the progressive stages of insight of the Mahayana. This is an experiential journey that offers a transformative understanding of reality.

———

As I reflect on what I have written, it's obvious that this approach to the buddhadharma is unorthodox. Some people may feel that it's a dog's breakfast of bits and pieces from east and west. I might even be accused of throwing the baby out with the bathwater.

While my approach is unorthodox, it is not disrespectful. I have abandoned traditional presentations only where they no longer seem culturally relevant. I have brought in contemporary elements where they seem to address vital contemporary issues. The choices were never frivolous. I have confidence that this inner path is the way of the Buddha.

This book is deliberately presented in bite-size pieces. I encourage you to take your time, absorbing and reflecting on the progressive stages of the presentation. Reading this kind of material quickly can be like trying to eat all of a day's meals in one sitting. You'll feel bloated and dissatisfied to boot.

My heartfelt wish is that this book will go a little way toward repaying the immense kindness of my teachers; that these teachings will provide you with new insights and inspiration; and that authentic Mahayana dharma will flourish in the modern world.

PART ONE

Starting from Square One

In which we prepare for an exciting and challenging expedition by verifying that our maps, compass bearings, and navigational instruments are in order. We make sure we have good methods for traversing different types of terrain and acquire provisions for the journey. And we set out.

1

Four Truths for Noble Beings

It's always best to start at the beginning, and all you do is follow the Yellow Brick Road.

—*Glinda, the Good Witch of the North,*
in The Wizard of Oz

SHAKYAMUNI, the buddha of this age, presented the core of the realization of all the buddhas when he first turned the wheel of dharma at the Deer Park in Rishipatana (the present-day city of Sarnath). In English, and other Western languages, these teachings have come to be known as the *four noble truths*. That has a nice ring but doesn't quite convey the meaning of the original. It is not the truths that are noble but the ones who realize them.

The four truths are: the *truth of suffering,* sorrow, or dissatisfaction; the *truth of the origin,* or cause of suffering; the *truth of cessation,* or the ending of suffering; and the *truth of the path* leading to the cessation of suffering.

In simple terms, the four truths consist of two pairs of causes and results:

-   the truth of suffering and its causes, and
-   the truth of the ending of suffering and its causes.

If we clearly saw what caused misery and what caused the ending of misery, we'd be fools to choose the causes of misery. We are not that stupid! The point is that we don't see these relationships correctly. We mistake causes of misery to be causes of happiness and endlessly chase after them, circling round and round in the wrong direction.

That is why it is more appropriate to refer to these teachings as the *four truths for noble ones*. These noble ones are the buddhas, the bodhisattvas, and the arhats who have attained direct insight into the nature of reality. They are the ones who clearly see these truths and act accordingly.

Why is this important? Because it points to how deep the four truths are, and how difficult they are to realize. It's not too hard to get a basic intellectual understanding of them, but that's only the beginning.

Suffering

When you're going through a difficult period in your life, the first truth, the truth of suffering, might really resonate with you. When things are going well, it's a lot harder to relate to it. The point of this first truth is that *all* our experiences are tinged with suffering and dissatisfaction. Sometimes this is blatant. At other times it is quite subtle—just a subliminal flicker of unease. We usually aren't aware of it, but even our peak experiences of joy and pleasure are tainted with the need to confirm how good the experience is, yearning for that joy and pleasure to continue, and subconscious fears that it will not.

Suffering's Cause

In the Foundational Vehicle, the causes of suffering are said to be craving and attachment. From the Mahayana perspective, this is where things get interesting. It is certainly true that craving and attachment are the causes of suffering, but as you begin to look deeply at craving and attachment, you see that the objects of craving and attachment are not the material, or psychological, or spiritual things we think we crave or try to cling to. The objects of this craving and attachment are our own projections—our mental versions of these objects. They are more like dreams of those things than the things themselves. That's why possessing them always disappoints.

It might occur to you that a new home, a new relationship, or a new spiritual practice would improve your life considerably. You start hankering after this acquisition, and mental images of the object appear to you again and again. As you ponder the possible qualities and defects of what you crave, you don't realize that it is the mental images—your own projections—that are driving the show. You also don't realize that the self that is doing the craving is also a projection: a collection of mental images. Looked at from this perspective, the fundamental cause of suffering and dissatisfaction is ignorance: not recognizing the nature of what you are experiencing.

Suffering's Cessation

The third truth, the truth of cessation, means we are not condemned to suffering without end. It is definitely possible to find genuine peace. Shakyamuni described his realization as "Profound, peaceful, stainless, lucid, and unconditioned—Such is the nectar-like truth I have realized."[1] His enlightenment demonstrates each of us has the potential for fundamental transformation. Suffering can be transformed into its opposite—bliss, joy, ease.

You and I are fundamentally no different from the Buddha, but our true nature is currently shrouded by temporary obscurations. These veils are not part of our basic makeup, but they *are* deeply habitual. We are so habituated to experiencing the world through these delusions that they have become invisible to us. They seem to be part of the furniture of reality. However, the third truth teaches that these obscurations can be removed.

The obscurations are of two basic types: emotional veils and knowledge veils. Emotional veils are ego-clinging or self-cherishing, along with all of the self-centered thinking that arises from that. Knowledge veils are not recognizing the nature of the phenomena that appear in our minds, along with the countless ways we are bound and driven by these projections, just like dogs growling at their own reflections in a mirror.[2] These two obscurations form continually shifting patterns of delusion.

The Path to Cessation

If the Buddha taught only the first three truths and not the fourth, we'd be really screwed. We'd learn that there is suffering and that it has a cause. We'd learn that there could be cessation from suffering. But we'd have no idea what the causes of that cessation could be.

The fourth truth is the truth of the path: the cause for the cessation of suffering. Unfortunately, there is no generic "one-size-fits-all" version of the path. The path is made up of various trainings that purify our obscurations to reveal our true nature, buddhahood. It is always tailored to the needs of the student and the abilities of the teacher. Nevertheless, it invariably consists of three aspects: *shila*, which means conduct, discipline, or ethics; *samadhi*, which means meditation or concentration; and *prajna*, which means wisdom, knowledge, or discrimination. Different traditions put more emphasis on one or another of these trainings, but all three are essential for the path to be an effective remedy for suffering.

2

The Three Trainings

When we have faith in genuine dharma, it is a joy to
practice it. Initially, it may feel like an effort to practice
the teachings, but gradually we experience their benefit
and practice becomes joyful. We feel so lucky to have
found these teachings and to be able to practice them.

With this foundation, our ability to increase love
and compassion is limitless. Through developing love
and compassion we purify all of the negativity from
our mind-streams that comes from clinging to self.

With the knowledge that any circumstance in which
we find ourselves is not truly existent, every situation
is workable and provides an opportunity to practice.

—*Khenpo Tsültrim Gyamtso Rinpoche*[1]

IT TOOK ME A LONG TIME to appreciate the importance
of training in ethical conduct. When I began my Buddhist
journey, I, like many of my peers, was rebelling against what we
perceived to be the hypocrisy of conventional morality. The last

thing I wanted was another uptight ethical system. Eventually, I began to see that Buddhist training in conduct was not conventional morality but a powerful method for helping others, while undermining self-clinging and delusion. Of course, with its endless resourcefulness, ego can turn even the practice of ethical conduct into mere "virtue signaling." That's not a good look, and it counteracts the purpose of this training. Even thinking "My conduct is superior to someone else's" is a real problem.

Training in conduct is presented in stages as we journey along the path. The conduct of the Foundational Vehicle is based on renouncing any behavior that harms others, such as killing, stealing, lying, and sexual misconduct. When we believe our happiness is more important than the happiness of others, we don't worry about the ways our selfish behavior might harm them. Practicing this training goes against these deeply ingrained tendencies to put our own welfare above theirs. Renouncing self-cherishing behavior primarily reduces emotional veils.

Mahayana conduct includes commitments not only to not harm others, but to actively promote their welfare. This is based on bodhichitta, the awakening mind. There are two aspects of bodhichitta. Relative bodhichitta is the intention to attain enlightenment so that you can bring the powers and wisdom of buddhahood to the aid of suffering beings. Absolute bodhichitta is the realization of the true nature of the self and of all phenomena. This realization reveals our buddhahood and enables us to be of the greatest benefit. The basic Mahayana training in conduct is embodied in the paramita practices, the transcendent actions of bodhisattvas.

Paramita literally means "gone to the other shore." This is a metaphor for transcendent action, practices that transcend self-concern. For these actions to be transcendent, they need to be free from self-centered reference points: the thoughts of an actor, an action, and an object of the action. This conduct is aimed at removing both emotional veils and knowledge veils.

The ultimate Mahayana conduct is the fruitional conduct called the practice of pure perception, or the practice of illusory form. Pure perception is based on recognizing that whatever you experience is inseparable luminosity-emptiness. This is practiced by continually recollecting that the nature of thoughts, emotions, and sense perceptions is fundamentally pure, complete, and perfect—whether they are good or bad, pleasant or unpleasant, hopeful or fearful. Whatever you experience is equally the expression of wisdom. This has nothing to do with a Pollyanna-ish attempt to smooth over life's difficulties. It is the purity that Shunryu Suzuki Roshi referred to when he told his students, "Each of you is perfect the way you are . . . and you can use a little improvement."[2]

Training in pure perception purifies clinging to duality, which is the root of both the emotional veils and the knowledge veils.

While it may seem like these three levels of training are distinct systems of ethical conduct, the higher systems include the lower ones. You don't abandon one system to take up the next. The practices are cumulative. The renunciation of the Foundational Vehicle is joined with the benevolence and wisdom of paramita practice. The fruition of these naturally leads to the practice of pure perception.

Meditation

Meditation is the second training on the path. This is a vast topic, but all Buddhist meditations are based on two methods: resting the mind and looking at mind's nature. Meditation techniques range from extremely complex and outrageously exotic to almost nonexistent. But at the core of each method is resting, looking, or both.

The practice of resting the mind is called *shamatha*, which means calm abiding or peacefully dwelling. That sounds nice, but it is easily misunderstood. When you hear about peaceful dwelling, you naturally might assume that meditation brings peace and calm by getting rid of disturbing thoughts, feelings, and emotions. In fact, it is the opposite. The point of shamatha practice is to *make peace with* all the unsettling emotions and thoughts that you have been forever trying to get away from. This means learning to rest right within all the sadness, anxiety, fear, anger, depression, discomfort, discursiveness, and confusion that constitute the emotional veils and the knowledge veils. The practice of resting meditation is a way of making friends with the obscurations, rather than suppressing or fleeing from them.

The practice of looking at the mind is called *vipashyana*, which means clear seeing or insight. Once you can rest a bit with your thoughts, feelings, and emotions, you begin to examine your previously unexplored inner terrain. Through looking, you gradually begin to discern the nature of these phenomena and discover they are not what you thought they were.

As the practice of meditation develops, you practice shamatha and vipashyana together: alternately resting and looking. First you rest, and when mind settles a little, you look. When looking starts to get too active, you rest. As you see more, you understand that you need more resting to look further. More resting, then, inspires more looking, in a virtuous circle.

In the modern world, popular interest in meditation is growing dramatically, and the therapeutic and performance-enhancing benefits of meditation are starting to be widely accepted. Scientific studies are beginning to validate these claims, and mindfulness practices are being introduced into many walks of life.

This is something to applaud. The techniques that the mindfulness movement have adapted are offering real benefits to more and more people. However, from a Buddhist perspective, it's important to understand that meditation's impact on worldly performance and mental well-being are merely side effects. They might be beneficial side effects, but chasing after them will distract you from the main point. The purpose of the path is not to make you more comfortable or happier, though contentment, acceptance, and well-being are healthy, natural by-products of practice. Meditation's ultimate purpose—toward which this training is directed—is to eliminate suffering at its root by overcoming delusion and then using the wisdom and freedom that come from that to help others overcome their delusion.

Wisdom

The third training on the path, cultivating prajna, reveals the wisdom that sees all phenomena as they truly are, removing the obscurations and revealing our true nature. This wisdom is cultivated gradually. It begins with study, which clarifies the view and provides intellectual foundations for the path. Contemplation makes this understanding personal and brings about deeper understanding and more confidence in the view. Finally, meditation within the view developed by study and contemplation brings about direct experience and realization.

This progression is similar to the way that insight develops in our ordinary lives. Imagine that you are thinking about taking a vacation. Friends have told you about their wonderful trip to Japan (or another fascinating destination), and their stories intrigue you. You might begin to learn about Japan by searching websites for articles about the country or buying guidebooks to some of its regions and cities. You would read about Tokyo and Kyoto, about the temples and palaces, about hot spring towns and Japanese baths, about the nightlife and fashions, about the unfamiliar cuisines and traditional gardens, about Shinto, Zen, and Pure Land. This study would give you a lot of basic knowledge about the country.

After all this research, you would need to contemplate what types of things seem most attractive to you. Are you more interested in history, art, or contemporary lifestyle and culture? Are there specialized interests you would like to pursue? Would you like to try to experience traditional inns or stay in Western-style hotels? In this phase, you make a personal relationship with what you've studied, mixing it with your own experience and making decisions about what you would like to do.

When you've made up your mind about what you want to do, you decide on an itinerary, book your tickets, and make your reservations. Finally, you get on a plane and go. When you arrive in Japan, the concepts of what it is like fall away as you directly experience the country, its culture, and its people.

This is similar to the way prajna develops as you journey on the path: study, contemplation, and meditation work together to reveal the direct experience of the fruition.

3

Awakening

The basic idea of the sitting practice of meditation is
that it is what the Buddha did, and because of that, he
attained enlightenment. That's the basic point. And we
have been told how to practice that way too, so that in
turn, we can attain enlightenment.

—*Chögyam Trungpa Rinpoche*[1]

THE MAHAYANA SUTRA called the *Lalitavistara* (*The Play in
Full*) recounts in rich, beautiful allegory how Shakyamuni
manifested in this world and how he journeyed to enlightenment.

The sutra begins with the events surrounding the Buddha's
birth to Queen Mayadevi and King Shuddhodana of the Shakya
clan. It goes on to describe the pleasures of his upbringing in his
father's palace; the sojourns beyond the palace walls that introduce him to sickness, old age, death, and the spiritual path; and
his escape from the palace to begin his journey to awakening.

After leaving his princely life, the Bodhisattva (as he is called
until his enlightenment) follows two of the foremost spiritual

teachers of his day, quickly surpassing them in his practice but still not realizing his goal. He then exerts himself in extreme austerities for six years.

Again, failing to find liberation, the Bodhisattva concludes that the path of self-mortification does not lead to awakening. He then recalls an episode of spontaneous meditation and insight from his childhood:

Once, when I was sitting in my father's park under the shade of a rose apple tree, I rejoiced as I attained the first level of concentration, which is free from desires and negativities, endowed with good qualities, reflective, investigative, and full of joy born out of discrimination. I rejoiced as I attained the levels of concentration up to the fourth. That, indeed, must be the path to awakening, which can eradicate the arising of the sufferings of birth, old age, sickness, and death.[2]

Following this recollection, the Bodhisattva leaves the banks of the Nairanjana River and proceeds to the seat of awakening at the foot of the bodhi tree. After circumambulating the tree seven times, he arranges a seat of freshly cut grass and sits "like a lion, like a hero, in a powerful way, in a steady way."[3]

As he meditates beneath the bodhi tree, the Bodhisattva thinks to himself, "Mara is the supreme lord who holds sway over the desire realm, the most powerful and evil demon. There is no way that I could attain unsurpassed and complete awakening without his knowledge. So, I will now arouse that evil Mara."[4]

And so, Mara arrives, surrounded by his terrifying army of ferocious warrior-sons and beguiling, seductive daughters, to challenge the Bodhisattva and prevent him from reaching his goal. At this point in the *Lalitavistara*, Mara and his retinue are depicted as supernatural beings, but an earlier passage in the sutra reveals their actual nature.

In that passage, the Bodhisattva tells Mara:

A coward cannot defeat an army;
Armies conquer and win respect.
Yet a hero can defeat an army;
O Mara, I will easily defeat you.

Desire is your foremost army;
Discontent comes next.
Third is hunger and thirst;
Craving is your fourth army.

Fifth is dullness and stupor;
Fear is said to be sixth.
Your doubt is army number seven;
Anger and hypocrisy come eighth.

Ambition, greed, and wanting praise,
Fame obtained through deception,
Seeking to exalt oneself
And put down others:

This is the army of Mara,
The evil friend who inflicts torment.[5]

Mara's armies are nothing other than the Bodhisattva's own negative emotions. When finally they attack, their weapons transform into flower canopies, celestial palaces, and halos of light. This is an analogy for recognizing the true nature of painful projections—they become free of themselves when they're seen to be nothing other than empty luminosity.

Failing to unseat the Bodhisattva through fear, Mara next tries to obstruct him through hope. He sends his daughters—Craving, Delight, and Discontent—to stir up lust in the Bodhisattva and seduce him from his journey. As they display themselves before him, "The Bodhisattva just smiled with unblinking eyes. He sat there smiling, with calm senses, physically at ease, resplendent, without attachment, free from anger, and without delusion."[6]

Having overcome all hope and fear, the Bodhisattva looks deeply into the nature of reality. He sees the arising of fundamental ignorance, and from that the chain reactions of delusion that form the basis of samsaric existence. He then sees that wisdom reverses the samsaric chain reactions and leads to peace. This is the moment of his complete awakening. At this moment, he becomes the Buddha, the *Tathagata*, the Thus-Gone One.

Approaching Practice

I recount this history of the Buddha's awakening because it contains excellent guidance about how to practice meditation. The Buddha's heroic battles with the attacks and seductions of Mara are no different from the experiences you will have when you sit down face-to-face with the things you hope for and fear. The images that arise in your mind as you meditate will seem banal and prosaic compared to the superhuman descriptions of Mara's sons and daughters, but they are really no different. You may feel that you are far from ready to approach the seat of awakening, but that is not true. You can follow in the Buddha's footsteps.

Begin by remembering that your true nature already exists within you. You don't need to look elsewhere for freedom. You have probably had your own spontaneous glimpses of peace and insight. These are examples that point the way. Try to remember that the purpose of dharma practice is to reveal what you've always been. You are not trying to fabricate some ideal version of yourself.

When you practice, do it with confidence and steadiness. Have good posture without becoming rigid and inflexible. Take your seat with some strength and naturalness. Feel the ground beneath you, and hold your head and shoulders upright. When you walk, try to walk lightly, in a relaxed, natural way.

Recollect that you won't find realization by beating yourself up. As the Buddha discovered, self-mortification is not the path to liberation. You can be aware of your faults without indulging in endless self-criticism, which is just one of ego's games for maintaining control.

Try not to turn away from negative or fearful projections. You might even welcome them. Occasionally you might recognize that they are your own experience—just the play of your own mind. They seem like experiences of solid people and places in a solid and real world, but they are really made of the same stuff as the people and places you experience in dreams.

After hearing the story of the Buddha's awakening, you might feel frustrated that your projections don't immediately transform into flower garlands and celestial palaces. Just remember that we are deeply habituated to taking our thoughts to be reality. Getting to know the true nature of your projections is going to be a journey.

Finally, try not to be seduced by hopes, even the hope for progress on the path. These mirages can seem quite beguiling, but they are also just projections.

Meditation

The *Lalitavistara* does not tell us if Shakyamuni used any meditation techniques as he sat beneath the bodhi tree. My hunch is that he had exhausted all distractions by that point in his journey, so meditation techniques would have been superfluous. But for those of us who don't have a great deal of meditation experience, and who are easily distracted, it is really difficult to practice in that way. We need a minimum of technique to keep us on track.

I first learned to meditate from students of Suzuki Roshi at the San Francisco Zen Center. Later, I became a student of Chögyam Trungpa Rinpoche, who taught a slightly different version of the same basic formless meditation practice. I want to share this technique with you because it is an excellent practice for beginners, as well as for advanced practitioners who want to look deeply into their experience.

Begin by relating with your posture. Your body expresses your state of mind. The way you work with your body will, in turn, affect your mind. It doesn't really matter if you sit on a cushion on the floor or in a chair, as long as the seat allows you to sit upright. Begin each session by dropping into the feeling of your body. You might feel agitation and discomfort, or you might have a feeling of well-being. It doesn't matter. Just settle into whatever it is. You don't have to do this for a long time, just long enough to feel you've arrived and settled in.

Then straighten up a little, as though you are being pulled up from the top of your head. Do this without tensing up. One image that helps convey what this is like is that your spine should be nicely balanced, like a stack of coins. Have a good sense of head and shoulders.

Next, become aware of your breathing. Continue to breathe naturally, and as you exhale, go out with the breath. At the end of the exhalation, the breath will dissolve into the space in front of you. You dissolve with the breath into space. You can rest in that openness or reconnect with the feeling of being in your body. You don't need to follow the breath as it comes back in. When you next exhale, again go out with the breath. Try to do this in a relaxed way. You don't need to put 100 percent of your attention on your breathing. Something like 25 percent is enough. The idea of going out with the breath is that you become the breath; you are not watching the breath.

As thoughts come up, you will find yourself distracted from the breathing. Don't regard this as a fault. Noticing what arises in your mind is an essential part of the practice. You don't need to follow the trains of thoughts or try to analyze their contents. Take note of these distractions by mentally labeling them "thinking," and go out with the next exhalation. Whatever comes up in your mind—discursive thoughts, emotions, feelings of various sorts—it is all considered to be thinking. We label all of these movements of the mind thinking *to accept them*, not to reject them.

That's it! Exhaling, resting in space, thinking, coming back, and breathing . . . the thoughts come and go . . . you get distracted, you notice the distraction, and you are already back. This is the basic technique.

Trungpa Rinpoche said this about formless meditation:

This is the closest thing to doing nothing. It is not quite doing nothing, because of the technique, but at the same time it is close to doing nothing. If you try to hold yourself to doing nothing and controlling yourself, then you are struggling with yourself and your energy. So if you let go with the energy, which is breathing, then you learn how to ride the breathing, so to speak, how to go along with the energy . . . relaxation and other things become by-products. One does not have to try to achieve or try to be in a perfect, particular state at all.[7]

When people begin to practice formless meditation, they usually become aware of a great deal of mental activity that was previously going on subconsciously. This might make you feel that the practice is making you worse: that your mind is getting out of control and your thoughts are starting to run wild. Not true. Noticing all this mental activity is actually a positive sign. It means you are beginning to awaken to what has always been going on.

4

Textures of Feelings

I believe that understanding the subtle body and its
influence on our thoughts, actions, and particularly
our emotions is essential to understanding the layers
that obscure our ability to relate warmly and openly
to ourselves, others, and the conditions that surround our lives. Without understanding the subtle
body, moreover, most meditation practices become
simply exercises in extending our own comfort
zones, a series of techniques that result in preserving
the solid sense of "I."

—*Tsoknyi Rinpoche*[1]

IN THE MODERN WORLD we often treat feelings like distant relations whom we only acknowledge when we see their
posts on Facebook or Twitter. Some feelings seem like annoying
younger siblings, who won't leave us alone while we play a game
or watch a movie. We squeeze and cuddle other feelings like cute,
little infants—until they spit up on our nice, clean clothes. We

are heady people. There is so much emphasis on thinking in our upbringing that we are often numb from the neck down.

It's ironic that many of us are able to know our feelings intellectually but unable to feel them directly. How did we get here? This could go back to our childhood. Maybe our parents' love was conditional on our behavior and our achievements. They showered us with affection when we did well, withheld warmth or punished us when we didn't do well or misbehaved, or just ignored us altogether. Maybe we were rejected and bullied by the cool kids or frequently embarrassed in front of our peers. We might have been traumatized by life-threatening illness, or damaging relationships, or loneliness. Some of us experience prolonged stress that comes from pushing ourselves to please others. Some of us have unrelenting work and career pressures that put us continually on the defensive.

There is little in our culture that encourages us to relate to these painful feelings simply and directly—quite the contrary. We are taught countless methods for analyzing, rationalizing, and avoiding our feelings. Our lives are all about doing, accomplishing, making progress. However we might feel, we are taught: Just get on with it. Relating directly to feelings seems too intense, too sharp, too penetrating.

At the first glimmers of fear, agitation, or embarrassment, we learn to smother the feelings with discursiveness, anesthetize them with intoxicants, suppress them with ignorance, or turn to our various screens for distraction. Instead of feeling the feelings, we end up experiencing attenuated, conceptualized versions of feelings. The obstructed and congested feelings become fixed into distorted psychosomatic patterns that disturb our bodies and our minds. These become long-festering wounds that manifest as physical disorders and mental neuroses. These patterns color our outlook on life, our images of ourselves, and our relationships with the people around us. If the distortions and blockages are great enough, they can lead to breakdowns and even psychosis.

The intellect is incapable of healing these wounds. This is not something you can solve by figuring it out. You won't be able to loosen the knots or remove the blockages with the thinking mind because the thinking mind is part of the problem. It is only by entering directly into the world of feelings that healing can begin.

The Subtle Body

Feelings manifest in definite locations and travel along regular pathways in our bodies. These locations and pathways are sometimes called the subtle body, but they are not anatomical features or physical structures. You won't find them by examining the body under a microscope. Although meditators sometimes visualize the subtle body in various shapes and colors, the subtle body is not a collection of esoteric symbols hidden beneath the skin.

The subtle body is the locus of emotional experience. This is where you meet feelings face-to-face. But you won't be able to know the subtle body in an analytical way—"Is it real?" "Does it exist?" "What is it made of?" All these questions are part of the intellect's way of knowing. They prevent you from directly encountering feelings and the subtle body. The only way to feel the feelings is to drop thinking and let awareness rest gently on the textures of feelings themselves.

When you do this, the first thing you will probably experience is fear. This might deflect you and set off a chain reaction of emotionality and discursiveness. That's normal. You don't need to be afraid of the fear. Although it seems like experiencing fear will cause you harm, fear will not damage you. If it pushes you away, try to gently drop back into contact with the feelings of fear. Try to observe where the feelings are located. Examine the texture of fear and its dimensions. If the fear freaks you out, don't be discouraged. Be gentle. Give yourself time. You can learn to work with fear.

When you enter the world of feelings, you might experience numbness instead of fear. If you do, feel what the numbness is like. What is the texture of the numbness? Try to rest right within that.

You will encounter all sorts of feelings. Feel them. Don't try to know them or understand them with thinking mind. Touch them lightly. Settle with the feelings. Connect with them without narration or judgment of any kind. Just be, and let the feelings be.

The feelings might open up, but if you approach them with an agenda of making them change or transform, they will solidify and become harder and more persistent. The way to find freedom from difficult emotions is to find it right within the feelings themselves. When you see that you are trying to get rid of feelings, feel that impulse and let it go. Healing begins when you change your attitude toward difficult feelings and welcome them to stay as long as they like.

HOW TO PRACTICE

You can work with your subtle body, both within meditation sessions and in daily life. When you are meditating and notice feelings of discomfort, you can hit pause on the meditation technique and work with the feelings directly.

Begin the subtle body practice by dropping thinking and letting awareness rest directly on the feelings. Gently stay with the feelings if they push back. Rest with the feelings. If you find yourself distracted and lost in narration, judging or thinking about why you have these feelings, let go of the discursive activity and return to experiencing just the texture of the feelings.

Don't force anything. Recognize when you want to make the feelings go away or transform them into something more pleasant. Feel that, and then settle back into whatever you're feeling. If the feelings open up and relax, so be it. If they don't open up and relax, so be it. Just be with whatever is happening in the subtle body. When the feelings diminish or shift, go back to the meditation technique. If they don't diminish or shift, that is also all right. If you struggle with feelings, they only become more solid and painful.

When you are not meditating and difficult feelings arise, you might be tempted to ignore them and push through with whatever you are doing. Don't do it! It is far better to take at least a few moments to do this subtle body practice. If you are about to have a difficult conversation with someone, for example, it's natural to have uncomfortable feelings. If you try to suppress the feelings and get on with the conversation, the feelings will distort your perceptions and your communications. If you can spend just a couple of moments touching in with the subtle body, the feelings won't be driving the bus. That doesn't mean they will go away, but there will be some space around them and this will provide room for intelligence to arise so that you can really be with the other person.

Sometimes you will feel very stressed, and start reciting the mantra "So much to do, so little time." Agitation, anxiety, and speediness will build up in your subtle body. You might be able to temporarily relieve yourself of these feelings with exercise, yoga, or various pacifying and distracting activities, but once these feelings accumulate, if you don't work with them directly, they tend to persist. Acknowledging feelings is the first step in working with them. Once you acknowledge them, locate where they are in your subtle body, and spend time making friends with them with this subtle body practice.

5

Perception and Conception

Even though judgments or discursive thoughts are
only representations and not real in themselves, they
nevertheless present themselves as real. In other
words, the thought of an "apple" is not an actual apple;
it cannot be eaten. Nevertheless, we have an innate
tendency to construe our thoughts as real. Thus . . .
we "fuse" or meld our representations of reality with
reality itself. As a result of seeming to be real in this
way, thoughts often seem highly relevant to one, and
they thus draw one into a whole series of thoughts.

—*John Dunne*[1]

I'M SITTING IN ONE of my favorite Halifax restaurants. If
you ask me what I see, I would describe the scene something
like this: "Jenna, the young owner of the restaurant, is seating
customers as they come in. There's a group of hipsters sitting
at the communal table, engrossed in a very serious discussion.
My friend Terry and his wife are dining with another couple at

a nearby table. Some students at the bar are drinking and having a rowdy time. My partner, Lynn, is sitting across the table from me, looking lovely. A familiar-looking waitress is coming over to take our order."

Well, that's not really what I *see*. What I see is only shape and color and texture. "Jenna," "owner," "friend," "hipster," and all the rest, are things that I *think*.

The process of perception is much subtler than it appears to be. In the first moment, there is sense perception. In the second moment—almost instantly after the sensation—a conception arises. These two experiences mix together as though they are one thing. In the narrative above, I have taken the sense perceptions and the conceptions to be one, mistaking my conceptions to be part of the world.

When I look at Jenna, in the first moment, I only see shape, color, and texture. That's visual form, pure sensation. What appears is not *a woman* or *an owner* or *a restaurateur*. These qualities are appearing to thinking mind. They are objects that appear to conceptual mind. Thinking blends the perception and the concept together. This is *superimposition*: a conception is superimposed on a sense perception.

To get a feel for how conceptions appear, bring to mind one of your parents (one who is not presently with you). Examine what arises in your mind. You'll probably experience thoughts about that parent, but there will also be something that this thinking seems to be directed toward. There will be a vague mental image of the parent, most likely in front of you. Maybe it will be vaguely like an image from a photograph, or it might be an image from some past experience. The image might not be well-defined at all, just an abstract blotch. The mental image won't be like a visual image. Compare the mental image of your parent with something you can see visually.

Here's another example. Listen to your current environment. You might hear a car or a refrigerator or a bird chirping. Note how you mix perceptions with conceptions. You *hear* sounds. You *conceive* of cars, refrigerators, and birds.

The technical term for such a conception is a *generality* (or to use the awkward Buddhist philosophical lingo, a *generally characterized phenomenon*). Generalities are what we superimpose on sense perceptions.

These examples seem pretty innocent. No doubt Jenna also conceives of herself as "Jenna" and as the owner of the restaurant. You might wonder, What's the big deal? So what if we mix sensations with conceptions?

The first problem is that not distinguishing conceptions from perceptions prevents you from experiencing things with a fresh, beginner's mind.[2] In the restaurant scene I described, this might merely cause me to overlook some of the richness of a night out. But consider what happens when you encounter a more emotionally charged situation, such as meeting with enemies or with friends.

When you see someone whom you think of as an enemy, the concept drives you to act in a certain way, even if that is not the most skillful way of relating to them. By reacting to your conception of enemy, rather than the person before you, you might miss an opening to improve that relationship, or you might overreact and make things worse. Likewise, with someone you conceive of as a friend. When you react to your conception of friend, rather than to the person, you might take them for granted, and damage the relationship by being insensitive to how the person is feeling at that moment, or you might miss an opportunity to deepen the friendship.

Conceptions are like maps of the sensory world. They are abstractions. When you can distinguish sense perceptions from conceptions, you see both the road and the map. Some maps are well constructed and accurately reflect the terrain: that person in front of you might act the way you would expect an enemy or a friend to act. Some maps are distorted: the person might act quite differently than you expect. It's good to keep your eye on the road, even when you have some confidence in the map. There are countless stories of people running off the road while consulting their GPS.

Another problem is that superimpositions mask sense perceptions, dulling them, as though you are looking at an image through gauze or smudged eyeglass lenses. Generalities eliminate the brilliance of the sensory world. When you distinguish the sense perceptions from conceptions, the sensory objects will appear more vivid and richer in detail.

Finally, when you mix perception and conception and take them to be one thing, you are not seeing things the way they really are. Distinguishing them and recognizing the nature of each of them is glimpsing genuine reality.

Distraction and Meditation

In superimposition there is some connection between the sensory world and the conceptual world. However, much of the time, these two worlds go their separate ways. You might be brushing your teeth when images from an Instagram post arise in your mind, provoking extended discursive thinking about the contents of that post. Tooth-brushing continues in one world, while your attention is riveted to a succession of generalities in the other. When the worlds of perception and conception are not connected, that is distraction.

When we begin to practice shamatha meditation the extent of our distraction becomes really obvious. New practitioners often feel discouraged when they see how hard it is to stay with the technique and let their minds come to rest. They feel that they aren't meditating properly because they are continually distracted and can't stay with the method. They think they are failing at meditation. This is a misunderstanding. Instead of feeling discouraged, this experience should bring joy! Seeing your distraction is one of the more important insights a practitioner can have.

The practice of meditation helps you recognize the distraction that normally flies beneath your radar. When you recognize that you're lost in thought, you learn to let go and return to the sensory world (until the next generality arises in your mind and jerks you away). Gradually, if you continue to practice, you will learn to see distraction more quickly, and following the technique will become easier. You become more skilled at recognizing distractions and letting go of your conceptions.

At this point, it's important to not treat distraction like something that needs to be suppressed. Distraction is an opportunity to look further at what is arising in your mind. Surprisingly, one of the best times to do this is when you experience a painful emotion. Usually, hurt and angry or resentful feelings consume us. If you look directly at your experience at such a time, you will find yourself face-to-face with the source of your painful feelings. You think there is someone else causing you to feel wretched, but if you look directly at what is appearing before you, you might see that it's not the other person but a generality—your version, or projection, of the other. At that very moment, the cause of your pain is the map, not the actual terrain. Seeing this could give you some space to breathe.

6

Exorcising Ego

The true enemy is inside. The maker of trouble, the source of all our suffering, the destroyer of our joy, and the destroyer of our virtue is inside. It is Ego. I call it "I, the most precious one."

"I, the most precious one" does not serve any purpose. It only makes tremendous, unreasonable, impossible demands. Ego wants to be the best and has no consideration for anyone else. Things work fine as long as "I, the most precious one's" wishes are being fulfilled. But when they're not, and Ego turns on the self, it becomes self-hatred. That self-hatred will eventually burn the house down.

—*Gehlek Rimpoche*[1]

I DON'T KNOW WHAT the "voice in your head" is like, but mine is full of self-concern. It's also generally critical, indignant, and pushy. It's usually asserting my needs, while ignoring the needs of others. This reference point seems inescapable. George Harrison brilliantly portrayed the ego's ongoing mantra in his song "I Me Mine" on the Beatles' *Let It Be* album. It's worth listening to. It really captures ego's relentlessness.

Ego is a source of self-deception. It minimizes, overlooks, or makes excuses for our transgressions and faults, while magnifying or demonizing the faults of others. Whenever we break something or make some other mistake, the ego leaps to the rescue by finding someone else to blame. It also performs another function: shielding us from the difficult realities of life, such as the inevitability of aging, sickness, and death. Somehow the ego accomplishes all this while maintaining the fiction that it—the self—exists as something more than a mirage. What a talented fellow!

The ego's perspective is a fundamental distortion, reinforced by religious, philosophical, and cultural beliefs. We take it for granted that this perspective is valid, that it's based on something that really exists. We assume that there is a self, that "I" refers to something real. You may never have questioned this assumption, but clinging to this belief is the source of misery without end.

An excellent way to begin looking into this illusion is to ask yourself some simple questions: Can you decide not to think? Do you control what you think? Do the thoughts control you? Do you control your emotions? Do they control you?

If there really is a thinker (the self) that produces thoughts, it should be able to control the process. It should be able to decide whether to think or not. It should be able to choose what to think about and what not to think about. Likewise, for feelings and emotions. If an autonomous self produces feelings and emotions, it should be able to choose which feelings and emotions to feel. So why do you sometimes feel crappy?

Ego is a superimposition. We don't just project our conceptions onto the world outside. We also project them onto our inner experience. Unlike such concepts as "box" or "yellow," which get superimposed on a limited range of phenomena, "I" and "me" are applied quite liberally to all sorts of experiences.

> When thoughts arise, "I" is projected to be the thinker of those thoughts.
> When we are doing something, "I" is conceived to be the actor or doer.
> When we feel bodily sensations, "I" is assumed to be the possessor of that body.
> When emotions arise, "I" is thought to be the emotional one.
> When we see, hear, smell, or taste something, "I" is understood to be the experiencer.

In each case, we perceive one thing and conceive of another. We *perceive* thoughts, activities, emotions, and sensations. We *conceive* of the self.

India in the seventh century C.E. was a time of great flourishing of the buddhadharma. Two enduring Mahayana masterpieces survive from that period. Both texts focus on the two central concerns of the Mahayana: methods for developing wisdom and methods for developing compassion. Each of these texts calls out the problem of ego.

Shantideva's *The Way of the Bodhisattva*[2] is a lyrical instruction for training in compassion based on the wisdom of no-self. The harm caused by ego is highlighted in this seminal verse:

All the joy the world contains
Has come through wishing happiness for others.
All the misery the world contains
Has come through wanting pleasure for oneself.[3]

Chandrakirti's *Entrance to the Middle Way*[4] is a profound instruction for training in wisdom. It begins with an homage to compassion as the seed, water, and ripening of "the victorious ones' abundant harvest." Chandrakirti singles out the problem of ego in this verse:

Seeing with their intelligence that all mental afflictions and
    problems
Arise from the view of the transitory collection,
And realizing that the self is the object of that view,
Yogis and yoginis refute the self.[5]

In this verse, the "transitory collection" translates the Sanskrit term *skandha* (heap). The "view of the transitory collection" is the belief that the fleeting, kaleidoscopic display of forms, feelings, perceptions, mental formations, and consciousnesses—the five skandhas—constitutes a self. This view is both instinctive and conditioned. The basic sense of self comes from the innate dualistic feeling of a "me" inside and "objects" that are out there. Even beings without developed linguistic concepts, such as human babies and nonhuman animals, seem to exhibit this instinctive self-conception.

The concepts of the conditioned self are learned as we grow up. We absorb them from the culture we are immersed in. Some come from religious training. Some come from psychology or philosophy. These conditioned views reinforce the instinctive feeling of me-ness.

To disprove the self means to decisively recognize selflessness—that "I" and "me" are illusory. The way to realize this is by thoroughly investigating the illusion to see if there really is somebody home.

A Detailed Investigation

To begin the investigation, you need to know what the self would be like if you could find it. The self we imagine seems to be a real thing, not just a vague intangible. Real things have characteristics. They are unitary, independent, and lasting.

- **Unitary** means that the self is singular. You don't have a whole bunch of selves, competing with each other or taking turns being in charge.
- **Independent** means that the self is unchanged by causes and conditions. Thoughts, feelings, and perceptions are obviously affected by causes and conditions, but the self that experiences them is unchanging.
- **Lasting** means that the self you have now is the one you've had all your life.

Can you find any unitary, independent, and lasting thing within your experience that corresponds to this type of self? To gain confidence in selflessness, you will need to thoroughly examine your body and mind. A cursory examination will not get to the heart of the matter.

Earlier, I mentioned that shamatha refers to meditation techniques for resting the mind and vipashyana refers to meditation techniques for looking at that mind. These investigations of self and selflessness are vipashyana meditations. A skillful approach is to alternate shamatha and vipashyana, resting and looking. First you let mind rest, and when it settles a bit, you begin to investigate. When the looking starts to become discursive or agitated, then rest again. Try to do these investigations while you practice meditation, and carry the questioning with you after you finish.

Begin by searching to see if your body is the self. There are lots of different experiences that make up what is thought of as "body." You can see hands, torso, and feet. You can see reflections of your face, your front, and your sides. You can feel tactile sensations all over. Do any of these, or the whole collection of them, constitute the self? Look carefully. Remember, it is not what you conceive to be your body that you are inquiring about. You're looking for a real thing that could be the self, not just a conception.

Next search through the various feelings that arise. You can feel anger, sadness, joy, confusion. You can feel sleepiness and dullness, agitation and comfort. Some of these feelings seem to be momentary. Some of them seem to last for quite a while. Again, ask yourself, do any of these feelings, or the whole collection of them, constitute the self?

Next investigate the mind. (This might appear to be the most logical possibility.) There are all sorts of moments of consciousness: consciousness of sights, consciousness of sounds, consciousnesses of feelings, and so on. Individually and collectively, do these consciousnesses have the unity, independence, and lasting characteristics of a self? Do you experience any-thing like a master consciousness that these consciousnesses are all part of?

These are difficult investigations. You will, no doubt, experience resistance from ego in the form of irritation, boredom, and distraction. That's to be expected. Don't be discouraged, but gently persist. I'm sure you will be rewarded by glimpses of selflessness.

A Logical Inquiry

The way we think about the self is slippery. Sometimes we take the body/mind to be identical with the self, thinking, for example, "I am sick" or "I am happy." Sometimes we take the self to be the possessor of body/mind, thinking, "I have a good feeling" or "I have a headache." Sometimes the body/mind seems to support the self; for example, "I am in my body," or "My mind resides in my brain." Sometimes the self seems to support the body/mind; for example, "My body is part of me."

This flexibility certainly helps to maintain the illusion that the self truly exists. We can use logic to begin to pin things down to simplify the search; the self is either the same as the body and/or the mind or something altogether different from either or both of these. The previous investigation examined whether the self was identical with the body/mind. Now you need to investigate the possibility that it is something altogether different from the body or mind. What on earth could such a self be like? It would not have any of the characteristics of either the body or the mind. Such a self would be inconceivable. How can you say that something inconceivable exists and that it is the basis for what seems to be so obvious?

A Thoroughgoing Search

It's commonly accepted that someone must be writing these words. If you ask me, I would say that I am writing them. But when I look closely, I can't find the writer. Thoughts that seem like words ripple in my mind. Conceptions of chapters bloom and fade. I see fingers moving across the keyboard of my laptop. Black shapes of letters and words appear on a white screen. That's it.

When you are reading these words, can you find a reader, or do you just experience the sight of text and the mental sounding of words?

If the self really exists, and it is involved in all these processes, you should be able to identify a distinct self, apart from the mere appearances of forms, feelings, perceptions, mental formations, and consciousnesses. Do you find such a self?

Finally, search for the searcher. What is it that is looking for the self?

———

When you get some understanding of selflessness, it will still be hard to break the spell of the illusion. The habits of ego are extremely deep. By investigating again and again, you will gain certainty in selflessness, and that will begin to weaken ego's hold.

> People may say that there aren't any tigers
> In a place where they are rumored to be.
> But you may not feel convinced that this is true.
> Instead, you may be disturbed by doubts about it.

But when you yourself have traced the root of mind
And have arrived at certainty about it,
It is as if you had gone to a place where tigers are said to
    live,
And had explored the whole region from top to bottom
To see for yourself if there were any tigers.
When you don't find any, you are certain,
And from then on have no doubt about whether or not
    tigers are there.[6]

An Interlude

THE FIRST LAW OF PHILOSOPHY: For every philosopher, there exists an equal and opposite philosopher.

The Second Law of Philosophy: They're both wrong.

PART TWO

Overcoming
Materialism

In which we proceed on our journey and overcome a major obstacle: the treacherous minefield of hidden assumptions.

7

Through the Looking Glass

Though there are areas of life and knowledge outside the domain of science, I have noticed that many
people hold an assumption that the scientific view of
the world should be the basis for all knowledge and all
that is knowable. This is scientific materialism.

Underlying this view is the assumption that, in the
final analysis, matter, as it can be described by physics
and as it is governed by the laws of physics, is all there
is. Accordingly, this view would uphold that psychology
can be reduced to biology, biology to chemistry, and
chemistry to physics. My concern here is not so much
to argue against this reductionist position (although I
myself do not share it) but to draw attention to a vitally
important point: that these ideas do not constitute
scientific knowledge; rather they represent a philosophical, in fact a metaphysical, position. The view that
all aspects of reality can be reduced to matter and its
various particles is, to my mind, as much a metaphysical position as the view that an organizing intelligence
created and controls reality.

—His Holiness the Fourteenth Dalai Lama, Tenzin Gyatso[1]

I F A FISH COULD TALK and understand human language, and if you could ask it what living in the water is like, I doubt it would have any idea what you were talking about. Water is the medium that fish live in, just as air is the medium we live in. It's something that we take for granted, and I imagine the same is true for fish.

Just like living in a physical medium, we are immersed in a cultural medium, a contemporary worldview that includes strong assumptions about the nature of mind and the natural world. For example, Cartesian dualism—the belief that mind and body are two completely different things—seems to be generally accepted as common sense. A conflicting assumption, that the mind is just the brain, seems to also be broadly accepted. We absorb these views about reality by osmosis from the culture we swim in. We tend to take them for granted, the way fish take water for granted.

Modern culture is dominated by science and technology. The empirical and theoretical methods of science have been incredibly successful in mastering the physical domain. They have given us unparalleled power over nature. Modern medicine has vanquished many of the ills of the past and vastly extended our life spans. Computers and the internet give us access to unbelievable amounts of information, extraordinary abilities to collect and analyze data, and endless possibilities of interacting. Industrial technologies exploit natural resources on a vast scale and transform them into an amazing diversity of products, to be consumed by billions of people. The development of atomic weapons has even given us the power to extinguish human life altogether.

Science has been so successful at mastering the physical domain, from the microcosmic to the cosmic, that it is hardly surprising that people feel that all truth must be based on science.

However, there is a domain of knowledge outside of the physical domain.

Science has very little to say about the mind itself, despite the tremendous amount of theorizing and scientific research about brain functions that's been done in recent years. In fact, it is hard to imagine how the third-person methods of science will ever be able to find purchase in the subjective realm. Yet it is commonly assumed that by explaining the brain, science will be able to explain the mind.

The Mental Domain

The introspective, philosophical, and ethical methods developed by Buddhists over the past 2,600 years have been incredibly successful at mastering the mental domain. They offer practitioners ways of taming the mind, developing empathy and compassion, and transforming obscurations into wisdom. Ultimately, they even lead to the complete extinction of delusions and suffering.

The mental domain is central to the Buddhist project. Delusion and suffering are mental phenomena. The extinction of delusion and suffering is Buddhism's raison d'être. Liberation does not come about through an external agent. It comes about through recognizing the true nature of mind. When you don't recognize the nature of thoughts, feelings, and emotions, you are deceived by them and ceaselessly driven by your own projections. When you do recognize their nature, you are freed from this compulsion.

Not recognizing the true nature of mind is like peering through a plate glass window from the wrong angle trying to see if your friends are sitting inside a restaurant. All you see is reflections of the outside. From that angle, you won't be able to tell if your friends are there or not, no matter how hard you look. Trying to eliminate delusion and suffering from the physical domain is approaching things from the wrong angle.

Opening the Door

Holding tightly to materialistic beliefs, which take the physical domain to be the dominant or exclusive reality, shuts the door to the realm of mind. That's why it's essential to surface these beliefs and challenge their validity. Implicit in these views is the assumption that whatever is mental has no causal capacity—that the mind is the brain and that the mental domain can be reduced to the physical domain. Some materialists even assert that the mental domain is completely illusory: that whatever is not established by science does not exist.

In the past, I have relied on traditional Buddhist teachings to overcome these reductionist views.[2] I now have doubts about the adequacy of this approach for people living in the modern world. Materialistic assumptions undermine the power of the buddhadharma by dismissing the importance of the mental domain. There isn't much ammunition in Buddhism to counter such metaphysical beliefs since they are inextricably tied to contemporary opinions about science and technology.[3] Fortunately, materialist dogmas are being challenged from within modernity itself. I believe, that if Buddhism is to come to terms with modernity, we must use the tools of modernity to address the metaphysics of materialism head-on.

Particularly during the past couple of decades, powerful voices within the philosophy of mind have begun to contest these reductionist views. This has led to a fascinating and illuminating debate. Even though the language of philosophy is quite different from the language of buddhadharma (and sometimes quite impenetrable to the uninitiated), don't think of this as a detour from our journey. We can use it as another way to investigate the nature of our projections, and the nature of reality.

If just the mention of the word *philosophy* makes you nervous and uptight, you can relax. I'll stick to clear, straightforward English as we explore what these thinkers have to say.

8

The Hard Problem

We have at present no conception of what an
explanation of the physical nature of a mental
phenomenon would be. Without consciousness the
mind-body problem would be much less interesting.
With consciousness it seems hopeless. The most
important and characteristic feature of conscious
mental phenomena is very poorly understood. Most
reductionist theories do not even try to explain it.
And careful examination will show that no currently
available concept of reduction is applicable to it.
Perhaps a new theoretical form can be devised for
the purpose, but such a solution, if it exists, lies in
the distant intellectual future.

—*Thomas Nagel*[1]

IN APRIL 1994, at the first Tucson "Toward a Science of
Consciousness"[2] conference, a young Australian philosopher
named David Chalmers delivered a talk that has shaped the con-

tours of contemporary philosophical debates about the nature of mind for the past quarter of a century.[3]

Chalmers was brilliant, funny, and a little awkward. His message, which he elaborated in a paper entitled "Facing Up to the Problem of Consciousness,"[4] was that there are two vastly different problems of consciousness. There are the *easy problems* that are accessible to the methods of cognitive science and neuroscience, and there is the *hard problem* of understanding subjectivity, or phenomenal experience. Chalmers noted ironically that the easy problems might take a couple hundred years to solve, but in principle third-person scientific methods should be up to the task.

The easy problems are easy because they involve explaining functions; for example, our ability to discriminate and react to the environment, the way information is integrated within the brain, and how we can report our mental states. To explain these processes, we only need to describe neural or computational mechanisms that can perform these functions.

If we want to explain vision, for example, we can show that light reflecting off objects is focused onto the retina within the eye, causing various cells to fire. These signals are encoded in the optic nerve, and they progress through various levels of processing on the way to the visual cortex in the brain, and so on. Eventually, we will have a complete picture of the way visual information is sensed and processed. But this will still leave the hard problem: How does all this processing lead to the phenomenal experience of seeing?

In "Facing Up to the Problem of Consciousness," Chalmers introduced the hard problem in this way:

The really hard problem of consciousness is the problem of *experience*. When we think and perceive, there is a whir of information-processing, but there is also a subjective aspect. As Nagel (1974) has put it, there is *something it is like* to be a conscious organism. This subjective aspect is *experience*. When we see, for example, we experience visual sensations: the felt quality of redness, the experience of dark and light, the quality of depth in a visual field. Other experiences go along with perception in different modalities: the sound of a clarinet, the smell of mothballs. Then there are bodily sensations, from pains to orgasms; mental images that are conjured up internally; the felt quality of emotion, and the experience of a stream of conscious thought. What unites all of these states is that there is something it is like to be in them. All of them are states of experience.

It is undeniable that some organisms are subjects of experience. But the question of how it is that these systems are subjects of experience is perplexing. Why is it that when our cognitive systems engage in visual and auditory information-processing, we have visual or auditory experience: the quality of deep blue, the sensation of middle C? How can we explain why there is something it is like to entertain a mental image, or to experience an emotion? It is widely agreed that experience arises from a physical basis, but we have no good explanation of why and how it so arises. Why should physical processing give rise to a rich inner life at all? It seems objectively unreasonable that it should, and yet it does.

If any problem qualifies as *the* problem of consciousness, it is this one.[5]

What is the connection between the subjective realm of experience and the realm that is described by science? These realms seem completely distinct. Do we have any way of connecting these dots? There are no commonly accepted scientific theories that explain this connection, and there may be principled reasons why this relationship just cannot be accommodated within physics as it currently stands. This gap in our understanding of the relationship of mind to the natural world has been called the *explanatory gap*.[6]

Many attempts have been made to bridge this gap. Some scientists have pointed to quantum mechanics and microstructures in the brain as possible sources of consciousness. Other researchers have suggested oscillations at 35–75 hertz in the cerebral cortex as the basis of consciousness. Still other investigators have proposed a global workspace within the brain as the place where information becomes conscious.[7] However, all these proposals fall short of traversing the gap. As Chalmers writes:

> The ambiguity of the term "consciousness" is often exploited by both philosophers and scientists writing on the subject. It is common to see a paper on consciousness begin with an invocation of the mystery of consciousness, noting the strange intangibility and ineffability of subjectivity, and worrying that so far we have no theory of the phenomenon. Here, the topic is clearly the hard problem—the problem of experience. In the second half of the paper, the tone becomes more optimistic, and the author's own theory of consciousness is outlined. Upon examination, this theory turns out to be a theory of one of the more straightforward phenomena—of reportability, of introspective access, or

whatever. At the close, the author declares that consciousness has turned out to be tractable after all, but the reader
is left feeling like the victim of a bait-and-switch. The hard
problem remains untouched.[8]

Inside Out

Attempting to bridge the gap from the introspective side of the
abyss seems equally daunting. We generally assume that the
brain must be the basis of the mind, and we know that there are
many correlations between brain activity and mental activity,
but when you look at your own mind, this connection isn't at
all obvious.

You can begin investigating this for yourself by looking at
your thoughts. Thoughts seem to arise in your head, but when
you look carefully, you see that thoughts do not come from anywhere and they do not go anywhere. You don't find any connection between thoughts and the brain. You can't find a structure
that the thoughts arise from, and the thoughts themselves do not
have any color or shape or form.

The same is true for emotions. Emotions also don't come
from anywhere or go anywhere. If you feel anxiety, you will feel
pain or discomfort that seems to be located in the center of your
torso. But when you investigate these feelings, you will not find
any connection to your physical heart. You won't find any anatomical structure that the emotions arise from, and the emotions
themselves don't have any color or shape or form.

You might feel that at least sensory experience provides an
unambiguous bridge between mind and the material world, but
let's take a look at that. Earlier in this chapter, we described vision

from the third-person perspective. Now let's look at it from the first-person perspective.

We often use the analogy of a camera to explain vision, but there is a fundamental difference between the way a camera functions and the way the eye and mind function. In a camera, the lens focuses the image on the sensor (or for old-school types, on the film plane). The camera's electronics digitally map this image onto a memory device. We then use this digital map to make viewable images on screens and occasionally to make paper prints. In each case, the image is separate from the objects being photographed.

The eye also focuses images on a sensor—in this case, the retina—and the image is mapped to electrical signals in the nervous system. However, instead of creating images that are separate from the objects being seen, the image appears in the space in front of us—right where the objects are assumed to be! In fact, the image seems to *be* the objects themselves. Normally, we take this for granted, but when you think about it, this is really weird. Why doesn't the image appear where the light is sensed within the eye? Ask yourself, What am I seeing? Is it objects in front of me, or images projected into the space of my mind?

The experience of hearing is similarly uncanny. We know that sounds are produced by changes in atmospheric pressure on the eardrum, yet the sounds are not perceived to be within the ear but in the space where they seem to originate. How is that possible?

We believe that we experience "a world outside," but this world of experience is always within our subjectivity. No matter where you look in the expanse of mind, you don't find anything physical. It's experience all the way down.[9]

The Mind-Body Problem

The hard problem/easy problem formulation is a refinement of the classical mind-body problem, which goes all the way back to Plato and Aristotle. It is a formulation that is well suited to this scientific era, which is why it has gained such traction. Despite the many, many advances of science, this way of understanding the issues shows that the hard problem is still with us.

As we investigate these issues, it is helpful to remember that the mental domain is not only fundamental to the Buddhist project but also fundamental to science. All scientific observations and theories occur within the mind. Without mind there would be no science. Here is a great irony: just as the eye cannot see itself, the objective methods of science cannot examine the knower of science—the subjective experience of the mind itself.

9

Eliminative Materialism

There occurred in the twentieth century the most
remarkable episode in the whole history of ideas—
the whole history of human thought. A number of
thinkers denied the existence of something we know
with certainty to exist. They denied the existence of
consciousness, conscious experience, the subjective
qualitative character of experience, the "phenomenal"
(or phenomenological) "what-it-is-like" of experience.
Others held back from the Denial, as I'll call it, but
claimed that it might be true—a claim in no way less
remarkable than the Denial.

—*Galen Strawson*[1]

MATERIALISM (OR PHYSICALISM) is the belief that
everything is physical,[2] that all thought, feeling, emotion,
and consciousness can be fully explained in terms of physical
phenomena—the particles and forces described by the laws and

principles of physics. Materialism comes in a variety of flavors. The most extreme version is called *eliminativism*:

> Eliminative materialism (or eliminativism) is the radical claim that our ordinary, common-sense understanding of the mind is deeply wrong and that some or all of the mental states posited by common-sense do not actually exist and have no role to play in a mature science of the mind.[3]

This approach attempts to resolve the hard problem by denying that there is anything about consciousness that needs to be explained, other than behavior and cognitive functions, eliminating the hard problem altogether.

Daniel Dennett, a philosopher and highly acclaimed author, is the standard-bearer for the eliminativist position. In his 1991 bestseller *Consciousness Explained*, Dennett sets out the eliminativist agenda:

> The idea of mind as distinct in this way from the brain, composed not of ordinary matter but of some other, special kind of stuff, is dualism, and it is deservedly in disrepute today. . . . The prevailing wisdom, variously expressed and argued for, is materialism: there is only one sort of stuff, namely matter—the physical stuff of physics, chemistry, and physiology—and the mind is somehow nothing but a physical phenomenon. In short, the mind is the brain. According to the materialists, we can (in principle!) account for every mental phenomenon using the same physical principles, laws, and raw materials that suffice to explain radioactivity, continental drift, photosynthesis, reproduction, nutrition,

and growth. It is one of the main burdens of this book to explain consciousness without ever giving in to the siren song of dualism.[4]

David Chalmers, and the hard problem of consciousness, are Dennett's bête noire: "I have been arguing for decades that Chalmers was mis-focusing our attention, exaggerating an artifact of inquiry that I identified in 1991."[5] In his voluminous writings on consciousness, Dennett tries to do away with the hard problem by claiming that subjectivity is a "multi-faceted illusion, an artifact of bad theorizing,"[6] somehow overlooking the fact that illusions are mental phenomena.

Dennett, and other eliminativists, use analogies to support their views, comparing the mystery of subjectivity to other mysteries that were later explained scientifically. Dennett uses the example of *vitalism*, the theory that explaining life required a special force or principle, distinct from purely chemical or physical forces. This theory was abandoned when such basic living processes as reproduction, metabolism, growth, and environmental adaptation were shown to have purely biological explanations. Dennett argues by analogy that, with further scientific research, the mysteries of consciousness will go the way of vitalism's élan vital.

Chalmers counters that this analogy fails because the mysteries of life that vitalist theories tried to address were always questions of function and structure, questions that physicalist explanations are well equipped to address, just as the easy problems of consciousness are functional and structural. What makes the hard problem hard is that there are no convincing functional or structural explanations for subjectivity.

Dennett's materialist convictions lead him to concoct a third-person methodology to explore consciousness and dismiss first-person perspectives as illusions, thus eliminating all subjective data from his philosophical program. He builds his physicalist case with evidence from the cognitive sciences—from computer science and what he calls "heterophenomenology"—his method of working with first-person experience from a third-person point of view. Essentially, Dennett takes people's reports of their mental images, pains, perceptual experiences, and so on and treats them as "theorist's fiction," which he claims is explained by his theories. By excluding the first-person perspective of experience as unscientific, he can study what he calls consciousness by examining people's beliefs and reports about their experience rather than subjective experience itself.

This feels like sleight of hand, where a magician substitutes a card he knows for the one you have chosen from his deck. People's beliefs and reports about conscious experience are not the hard problem that needs to be explained. It is difficult to see how heterophenomenology, a third-person perspective, can substitute for phenomenology, *real first-person experience.*

Dennett's (Quasi)-Buddhist Insight

Central to Dennett's theory of mind is an insight that resembles a key Buddhist insight: selflessness, or the lack of any central reference point. The Buddha realized selflessness by investigating the nature of his own phenomenology. Dennett developed this insight from studying neurophysiology. This is his assessment:

There is no single, definitive "stream of consciousness," because there is no central Headquarters, no Cartesian Theater where "it all comes together" for the perusal of a Central Meaner. Instead of such a single stream (however wide), there are multiple channels in which specialist circuits try, in parallel pandemoniums, to do their various things, creating Multiple Drafts as they go. Most of these fragmentary drafts of "narrative" play short-lived roles in the modulation of current activity but some get promoted to further functional roles, in swift succession, by the activity of a virtual machine in the brain.[7]

Dennett's Multiple Drafts theory sounds like the Buddhist description of the skandhas, the ever-changing "heaps" of experience that we mistake to be a self. My hunch is that Dennett has understood something about the illusory nature of the self—something that all Buddhist schools would agree with—and conflated the self with consciousness.[8] That's the only way I can make sense of his belief that subjectivity is an illusion: he conflates *no subject* of experience with *no subjectivity*.

Buddhist practitioners, too, find it hard to imagine that there really is nobody home, and yet experience is unceasing. Accustomed as we are to believing that the self is the agent that causes thinking, perceiving, and feeling, it seems inconceivable that mind could continue to function without the self.

Yet the self never existed, and still there is subjectivity.

10

Reductive Materialism

Reductionism: One of the most used and abused
terms in the philosophical lexicon.

—*The Oxford Companion to Philosophy*[1]

ELIMINATIVISM IS deeply counterintuitive, but other materialist approaches are somewhat less dismissive of consciousness. Unlike eliminativists, who reject subjectivity outright,
reductionists accept that subjectivity is a phenomenon that needs
to be explained, but they believe the explanation will ultimately
be physical.

The term *reduction* is used in philosophy to describe how one
theory or phenomenon might be reduced to a more basic theory
or phenomenon. When one thing is reduced to another . . .

the thing reduced (referred to as the *target*)
fully depends upon or is composed of
the more basic thing (referred to as the *base*).

Saying that the target reduces to the base typically implies that the target is nothing more than the base. In other words, mind seems to be real, but it's actually just this or that physical process. It does not really perform the functions it seems to perform.

Reductive materialism is based on the claim that all sciences are ultimately reducible to physics. This is usually taken to mean that all phenomena, including mental phenomena, are identical to physical phenomena. Reductionists often argue that (at least in principle) biology can be reduced to chemistry, and chemistry can be reduced to physics. In the same way, they assert that consciousness can be reduced to physical processes.

One of the early reductionist approaches to consciousness was the *mind/brain identity theory*. The late Australian philosopher J. J. C. Smart was one of the theory's founders. His presentation of the core of this theory is a good example of the style of argumentation used by reductionists:

> The identity theory of mind holds that states and processes of the mind are identical to states and processes of the brain. Strictly speaking, it need not hold that the mind is identical to the brain. Idiomatically we do use 'She has a good mind' and 'She has a good brain' interchangeably but we would hardly say 'Her mind weighs fifty ounces'. Here I take identifying mind and brain as being a matter of identifying processes and perhaps states of the mind and brain. Consider an experience of pain, or of seeing something, or of having a mental image. The identity theory of mind is to the effect that these experiences just *are* brain processes, not merely *correlated with* brain processes.[2]

Identity theorists try to establish their theory by pointing to experimental observations. They say that whenever there are mental states, there are corresponding brain states. Having observed systematic correlations between mental events and neural events, they conclude that the mental and the neural are identical. They use Occam's Razor (the principle that theories with the fewest assumptions are most likely to be true) to support their approach. They argue that even though mind/brain correlations are compatible with other theories, the identity theory is the simplest explanation for these observations. They do not try to bridge the explanatory gap but claim, "That is just the way things are. Mental phenomena just *are* physical phenomena."

Functionalism is another reductive approach. Functionalists say that mental states can be characterized by their roles in psychological theories that explain the relationship of sensory inputs and other brain states to behaviors. These physical states are conscious because they play the right functional role in explaining behavior. Functionalists argue that their approach takes mental states out of the realm of subjective experience and makes them accessible to scientific investigation.

The *global workspace hypothesis* is a popular functionalist approach. Proponents of this theory say that conscious states are mental states that are available for processing by a wide range of cognitive systems because they are present in a special neurological network. Like identity theorists, functionalists do not attempt to bridge the explanatory gap. They simply say that fulfilling the appropriate function is what it means for something to be conscious.

There is another reductionist approach that consists of a range of different representationalist theories. Representationalists reduce consciousness to "mental representations" rather than directly to underlying states of the brain, but most representationalists believe that there is (or eventually will be) a second reduction to neurological states. These theorists argue that consciousness can be explained in representational terms and representation can be understood in purely physical terms.

There is another group of theorists worth mentioning, and these are the aptly named *mysterions*. Mysterions acknowledge the difficulty of the hard problem of consciousness and accept that current scientific theories do not provide convincing answers. However, they have faith in the naturalist project and believe that future scientific advances will be able to bridge the explanatory gap.

While the naturalistic approach of the sciences has been remarkably successful in other domains, it is ironic that some mysterions have blind faith in the ability of science to resolve the hard problem. There are other mysterions who lack such faith. They believe that while there must be a naturalistic solution to the hard problem, there are fundamental reasons why it will forever be beyond the cognitive abilities of humans to solve.

Phenomenal Concept Strategy

A general objection to all of the reductionist approaches is that they deny our intuitions about subjective experience without providing anything to bridge the explanatory gap. One reductionist response to this objection is what Daniel Stoljar (another Australian philosopher) called the *phenomenal concept strategy*. This approach argues that the reason there seems to be an explanatory gap is that our first-person concepts about phenomenal experience and our third-person concepts about physical processes are fundamentally different, but both are pointing to the same reality. First-person phenomenal concepts point to conscious experience in a subjectively direct manner. Third-person concepts point to the actual physical state of affairs. Because these are different modes of conceiving of the same things, consciousness does not intuitively seem to be physical, but this intuition is mistaken.

One problem with this phenomenal concept strategy is that much of our phenomenal experience is not conceptual at all. Take the experience of a headache. You don't need to think about whether or not your head aches. This is something you know directly, without having to conceive of it. You might have conceptions about the headache—"It's a really bad headache," "I shouldn't have had so much to drink last night," "I need to take something for this throbbing pain," "This philosophical stuff makes my head ache"—but you know the pain directly, nonconceptually.

Personally, I find it hard to resist the impression that all of these materialists are so blinded by their metaphysical assumptions that they take what cannot be doubted—the fundamental fact of experience, the experiencing mind, cognizance itself—and reduce it to their conceptual models: theoretical objects that exist in their minds. Perhaps the reduction needs to go in the other direction. Could these physicalist models be reduced to mere mental fabrications?

Recollecting the Context

At this point, you might be wondering, Why should we Buddhists care about any of this? It all goes back to the Mahayana understanding of the second truth for noble ones, the truth of the origin of suffering.

Craving and attachment cause suffering. There is one thing we cling to even more tightly than things we want and things we fear: that is our projected reality—what we take to be a material world existing independently of our minds, including our versions of "I," "me," "mine"—a world that we believe is experienced by everyone.

Clinging to these conceptions is the essence of materialism. If we're not able to challenge the reality of materialism and release our death grip on the mirages we project, we will never be able to find freedom or lasting peace. This is where the concern with materialism comes in. Believing in the true existence of extramental objects makes it extremely difficult to recognize the way we fabricate mental realities; we confuse projections for an independently existing world that has the capacity to bring us joy or sorrow. This delusion is the engine of samsara.

This is why we need to challenge materialist beliefs that are the glue that holds samsara together.

11

The Case against
Materialism

All the evidence available to us indicates that consciousness, including pure awareness, is contingent on
the brain. Nevertheless, my viewpoint isn't a materialist one, for two reasons. First, consciousness has a
cognitive primacy that materialism fails to see. There's
no way to step outside consciousness and measure it
against something else. Science always moves within
the field of what consciousness reveals; it can enlarge
this field and open up new vistas, but it can never get
beyond the horizon set by consciousness. Second,
since consciousness has this kind of primacy, it makes
no sense to try to reductively explain consciousness in
terms of something that's conceived to be essentially
nonexperiential, like fundamental physical phenomena. Rather, understanding how consciousness is a
natural phenomenon is going to require rethinking our
scientific concepts of nature and physical being.

—*Evan Thompson*[1]

W E'VE ALREADY TOUCHED ON the explanatory gap. This is an important argument against materialism. Simply put, if you can't explain the physical principles that connect mind and brain, how can you say that the mind is just physical, or reducible to the physical? We're now going to explore several canonical thought experiments that illuminate just how deep the explanatory gap is. I encourage you to contemplate these arguments for yourself to help investigate your own assumptions.

The Knowledge Argument

Frank Jackson's 1982 paper "Epiphenomenal Qualia"[2] presents what is called the *knowledge argument* against physicalism. A thought experiment in that paper describes a brilliant neurophysiologist, Mary, who lives sometime in the future and who has never experienced color. In the original version of the argument, Mary grew up in an entirely black-and-white environment. A modified version of the story (that avoids some technical difficulties with the earlier version) is that she was colorblind from birth. Mary learns the science of color vision: the physics, chemistry, and neuroscience. She knows everything that can be known about color vision—except for the experience of seeing color.

When Mary leaves the black-and-white environment, or when advances in medicine come up with a cure for her colorblindness, Mary has her first color experiences. When she sees a ripe tomato for the first time, she learns what red *looks* like.

As Jackson wrote:

It seems just obvious that she will learn something about the world and our visual experience of it. But then it is inescapable that her previous knowledge was incomplete. But she had *all* the physical information. *Ergo* there is more to have than that, and Physicalism is false.[3]

Materialists have argued against Jackson's conclusion in various ways, but it is clear that knowing all the scientific facts and theories about vision will tell you nothing about the first-person experience of seeing the color red. That experience is knowledge that cannot be derived from scientific information. Even though Mary already knew all the physical and biological facts about the color red, there was no way she could have known what it actually *looked* like.

Conceivability Arguments

When you and I look at a ripe tomato, we probably both think the color we are seeing is red. When we look at freshly mown grass, we think the grass is green. How do you know that we have the same phenomenal experience in each case? Perhaps my experience of red is your experience of green and vice versa. This scenario is what is called a *qualia inversion*. *Qualia* is the term philosophers use for all of the qualities that appear to our minds. They are what Buddhists refer to as *dharmas* or *phenomena*.

The conceivability of qualia inversions, first proposed by the philosopher John Locke in the seventeenth century, points out that none of our scientific knowledge can predict the qualia we experience. David Chalmers proposed an even more radical thought experiment along these lines. This is what's known as the *zombie hypothesis*. No, it's not the *Night of the Living Dead* kind of flesh-eating zombies. These zombies are physicalist-eating philosophical zombies. They are imagined to be beings who are physically identical to us, down to the molecular level, except that they lack consciousness. Their brain processes are just like ours. Their behavior is just like ours. Yet they do not experience anything. As Chalmers describes them, "all is dark inside." His conclusion from this thought experiment is:

> From the conceivability of zombies, proponents of the
> argument infer their metaphysical possibility. Zombies are
> probably not naturally possible: they probably cannot exist
> in our world, with its laws of nature. But the argument holds
> that zombies could have existed, perhaps in a very different
> sort of universe. For example, it is sometimes suggested
> that God could have created a zombie world, if he had so
> chosen. From here, it is inferred that consciousness must be
> nonphysical. If there is a metaphysically possible universe
> that is physically identical to ours but that lacks conscious-
> ness, then consciousness must be a further, nonphysical
> component of our universe. If God could have created a
> zombie world, then (as Kripke puts it) after creating the
> physical processes in our world, he had to do more work to
> ensure that it contained consciousness.[4]

The Primacy of Mind

The materialist thesis is that the physical world is the primary reality and that the mind is secondary (or even illusory). However, this overlooks the quintessential point: the objective world described by science is a mental construct. It is not "the world as it actually is." The belief that science reveals reality is more theological than scientific. This belief is *scientism,* or *scientific materialism.*

The French philosopher Michel Bitbol has traced the way scientific models of reality are constructed by abstracting from direct experience. This is my summary of his presentation:[5]

The process of abstraction begins with ordinary human experience. From this, features that are particular to individual observers are removed, and observations that can be broadly replicated are extracted. On the basis of these intersubjective observations, formal models are created, using mathematics and logic, that can be used to predict events, and these predictions are used to validate the models.

The way the concepts used in thermodynamics developed is a classic example of this process. Temperature, pressure, and volume all have experiential bases. Before these variables were extracted from experience, there were bodily sensations, ordinary practices for working with materials, and observations about the ways various substances expanded and contracted when they were heated or cooled. Heat and temperature were hardly distinguished from one another and from sensations of hotness and coldness. Pressure was a name for the feeling of something pressing against the skin.

Gradually, systems of quantitative values emerged from this experiential soup, together with laws that described the relations between the variables. Even though bodily sensations of hotness and coldness were still the experiential basis for temperature, they became less and less prominent as thermodynamic concepts became more and more comprehensive. Finally, the sensations of hotness and coldness were no longer implicit standards at all. They were replaced by the boiling point and freezing point of water, which became references for temperature scales in liquid thermometers. The visual experience of reading the temperature from various instruments was given priority over tactile experiences of warmth.

When you say, "I feel hot," this is indisputable, even when the temperature in the room is 10 degrees Celsius (50 degrees Fahrenheit, or for the truly nerdy, 283.15 Kelvin). But "subjective" feelings of hotness and coldness have become second-class citizens in the realm of knowledge. At this last stage of the process of objectification, experience is distrusted, even though perceptions and judgments are still the foundation that all knowledge rests on.

Bitbol goes on to remark:

> Now, the problem is that the very success of this procedure of extracting invariants yields a sort of *amnesia*. The creators of objective knowledge become so impressed by its efficacy that they tend to *forget* or to minimize that conscious experience is its starting point and its permanent requirement. They tend to forget or to minimize the long historical process by which contents of experience have been carefully selected, differentiated, and impoverished, so as to discard their personal or parochial components and to distillate their universal fraction as a structure. They finally turn the whole procedure upside down, by claiming that experience can be explained by one of its structural residues.[6]

Summation

The explanatory gap, the knowledge argument, conceivability arguments, the primacy of mind—all these point to the incoherence of the materialist conception of reality. But here's the kicker: Materialism is a way of *thinking* about reality. It is conception, a mental phenomenon.

Isn't that ironic!

Abstracting the Weather

I live in a place with a fairly long winter, followed by an even longer cold and wet season my friend Judith calls "sprinter." Around the middle of March, I start craving warm, sunny weather. I have four weather apps on my phone, and I've been known to consult them obsessively during this period. Usually, I'm oblivious to the amazing science and technology behind these forecasts—the atmospheric studies, the math, fluid dynamics, cartography, supercomputing, and so on. I just want to know how awful it's going to be outside and when we might finally get a little warmth and sunshine.

Perhaps my obsession with forecasts explains why I found Pico Iyer's piece "The Folly of the Weather Forecast" so striking.[7] Iyer writes:

> I never read weather forecasts. As soon as I read one, tomorrow is clouded for me, even if it is sunshine that's predicted. A part of me is making plans, or second-guessing the heavens; a part of me is saying, "I should be able to get in a second walk tomorrow, though by Sunday night it's going to

be cold again." When it turns out different, as it often will, all my thinking is in vain.

It isn't that weather forecasts mess with my mind. It's that the mind is so ready to mess with everything it touches—to make theories around it, to draw fanciful conclusions from it, to play distorting games of projection and miscalculation—that even the elements are not safe from it.

The difference between the fabricated reality of the weather forecast, and the actual experience of weather, is profound. The forecast is *useful*. It lets you know how to dress for the day, when you will need to water the garden, and if you should prepare for a dangerous storm. But the forecast also tends to obscure the experience of actual weather.

The actual experience of weather is *real*. It does not depend on imagination about the future. Science and technology are *useful*. But materialism tends to make you discount, or forget, the genuine reality of lived experience.

———

There are contemporary nonphysicalist views of mind and nature we could discuss, but it's time to proceed with our Mahayana journey. If you're interested in exploring some fascinating alternatives to materialism, appendix 1 offers a brief survey of the ways that philosophers currently think about this.

An Interlude

THERE'S AN OLD Jewish anecdote that goes like this. A pope in the Middle Ages decreed that all the Jews had to leave Rome or convert to Christianity. The Jews of Rome were distraught and outraged, and they demanded that the pope debate with their grand rabbi to prove the truth of their religion. The pope agreed and said that if the grand rabbi won the debate, the Jews would be allowed to stay. Since the rabbi did not speak Latin and the pope did not speak Yiddish, they agreed to hold the debate in silence, using only gestures.

The debate was to take place in a great Roman amphitheater. When the appointed day came, the pope, surrounded by his retinue of cardinals, entered from the western gate. The grand rabbi, surrounded by his retinue of rabbis, entered from the eastern gate. The two debaters sat facing each other, at either side of a long table, in the center of the arena.

This is what transpired:

The pope began by slowly sweeping his right hand over his head in a broad arc.

The grand rabbi responded by tapping the table with his right index finger.

Next, the pope held up three fingers.

The grand rabbi responded by holding up one finger.

Finally, the pope reached into his bag and pulled out a fish and placed it on the table. The grand rabbi responded by pulling an apple from his bag and placing it on the table.

Then they both arose and retired to their dressing rooms, surrounded by their anxious followers.

In his dressing room, the pope sat bolt upright as the cardinals flocked around him, clamoring to know what had happened. Finally, the pope spoke. "The grand rabbi is a very wise man. He defeated me at every turn. The Jews can stay." The cardinals cried out, "But what was the meaning of the signs?"

Then the pope explained, "I waved my arm to indicate that God is everywhere. The grand rabbi countered by tapping the table to indicate that God is right here. I held up three fingers to symbolize the Trinity. He responded with one finger pointing out their essential unity. Finally, I showed him a fish to signify our salvation through Jesus Christ, and he showed me an apple to remind me of original sin."

In his dressing room, the grand rabbi was banging his head against the table as the other rabbis flocked around him, demanding to know what had happened. Finally, the grand rabbi stopped hitting his head and moaned, "We lost . . ." The rabbis cried out, "But what happened? What was the meaning of the signs?" The grand rabbi explained, "First, he waved his arm, meaning, Jews get out of Rome! So I gave him the finger. Then he held up three fingers, meaning you've got three days to get out. So I said we're staying right here. Then he took out his lunch, and he had a fish. I took out my lunch, and all I had was an apple!"

PART THREE

A Profound Journey

In which we make a gentle ascent through the stages of insight into genuine reality, following the path of the Mahayana's historical development. Our journey concludes with some reflections on joining these insights with daily life.

12

Traces of the Buddha

"Whatever is conducive to liberation and not to
bondage"—so the Buddha is said to have told his
followers—"that is my teaching."

—*Jan Nattier*[1]

UNLIKE THE ABRAHAMIC RELIGIONS (Judaism, Christianity, Islam), Buddhism does not depend on historical revelation coming down through the ages to reveal the ultimate. The Buddha taught that each of us must find liberation within our own being. The Buddha was a human, who fully realized the profound truth and attained enlightenment. He was not a god or a prophet. He was a teacher and an example. The Buddhist teachings show how we can realize the same liberation that he realized.

One of the most well-known summaries of the Buddha's teachings comes from the *Sutra on Dependent Arising*:

All phenomena that arise from causes,
The Tathagata has taught their cause,

And that which is their cessation,

Thus has proclaimed the Great Renunciant.[2]

The point of the buddhadharma is to show us the causes of bondage and the causes of liberation. It is up to each of us to gather positive causes.

The sutras—recollections of the discourses of the Buddha and his immediate disciples—were originally oral accounts, composed by his followers in a formulaic and repetitive style to help them memorize these teaching narratives and pass them on. They were not written down until the second or first century B.C.E., hundreds of years after the Buddha passed into nirvana. Even after the early sutras were committed to writing, new sutras continued to appear for another millennium. Not surprisingly, the numerous texts in the Theravadin, Chinese, and Tibetan canons contain many layers of teachings from different periods, reflecting different ways of explaining the truth, as well as the different needs of practitioners, as societies and sanghas evolved through time.

The Mahayana did not arise in a vacuum. The roots of these teachings go back to the time of the Buddha. There must have been many teachings that were not recorded in the canons. Some of them would have been verbal, some only communicated through signs. The apocryphal "Flower Sermon" is what the Zen folks call "a transmission outside of the scriptures." It's a Chinese story that describes Shakyamuni wordlessly instructing the sangha by holding up a flower, while "subtly smiling." Only Mahakashyapa understood the transmission and smiled back. I imagine there must have been many such occasions.

Traditional descriptions of the origins of the Buddhist canon tend to smooth over, or ignore, these complexities. Some accounts say that Ananda, the Buddha's primary attendant, recited the sutras at the First Council, held soon after the Buddha's parinirvana (final nirvana—the state of nirvana a buddha enters at death), and that Upali, another main disciple of the Buddha, recited the Vinaya, the code of conduct. The assembled arhats accepted these versions of the teachings, and thus the canon was born, fully formed.

What the Buddha Taught

Contemporary scholarship, based on linguistic research, textual analysis, and archaeological evidence, paints a more organic picture of the development of the teachings. There is much uncertainty about what the Buddha actually taught, but it is clear that his central concern was guiding people on the path to liberation. It seems quite unlikely that he was interested in metaphysical speculation. The sutras contain lists of speculative questions that the Buddha famously refused to answer. Is the world finite or infinite? Is the world eternal or not? Are body and mind the same or different? Does the Tathagata continue after death? In answer to each of these questions, the Buddha remained silent.

There's a nice story in *The Shorter Discourse to Malunkyaputta* which tells of the monk Malunkyaputta coming to the Buddha and insisting that he will only continue to follow his teachings if the Buddha will answer such questions.

The Buddha tells him:

Malunkyaputta, if anyone were to say, "I won't live the holy life under the Blessed One as long as he does not disclose to me that 'The cosmos is eternal,' . . . or that 'After death a Tathagata neither exists nor does not exist,'" the man would die and those things would still remain undisclosed by the Tathagata.

It's just as if a man were wounded with an arrow thickly smeared with poison. His friends and companions, kinsmen and relatives would provide him with a surgeon, and the man would say, "I won't have this arrow removed until I know whether the man who wounded me was a noble warrior, a brahman, a merchant, or a worker." He would say, "I won't have this arrow removed until I know the given name and clan name of the man who wounded me . . . until I know whether he was tall, medium, or short . . . until I know whether he was dark, ruddy-brown, or golden-colored . . . until I know his home village, town, or city . . . until I know whether the bow with which I was wounded was a long bow or a crossbow. . . ." He would say, "I won't have this arrow removed until I know whether the shaft with which I was wounded was that of a common arrow, a curved arrow, a barbed, a calf-toothed, or an oleander arrow." The man would die and those things would still remain unknown to him.

In the same way, if anyone were to say, "I won't live the holy life under the Blessed One as long as he does not disclose to me that '"The cosmos is eternal,"' . . . or that '"After death a Tathagata neither exists nor does not exist,'" the man would die and those things would still remain undisclosed by the Tathagata. . . .

And why are they undisclosed by me? Because they are not connected with the goal, are not fundamental to the holy life. They do not lead to disenchantment, dispassion, cessation, calming, direct knowledge, self-awakening, unbinding.[3]

There have been countless arguments between Buddhist schools about the actual words of the Buddha, but we have no way of knowing which, if any, of the words attributed to him were actually spoken by him. We can only make educated guesses about which of the teachings in the sutras come from the very earliest strata.

The Buddha might well have taught certain core themes "connected with the goal" and "fundamental to the holy life." The four truths—suffering, the cause of suffering, the cessation of suffering, and the path—seem to be central to the Buddha's message, although perhaps not in the formulation that we have now. The three marks of existence—that whatever arises from causes and conditions is impermanent, selfless, and a cause of suffering—also seem to be essential. Applying the teachings of the three marks to the person, through the practices of contemplation and meditation, seems very basic. An overarching theme of the early teachings is that the path to liberation consists of the cultivation of virtue, the abandonment of nonvirtue, and taming the mind. Another basic theme is dependent origination: that causal chain reactions, beginning with ignorance, and continuing through *kleshas* (afflictions or defilements) and karmic action, always lead to suffering and bind us in samsara.

Abhidharma

What the Buddha taught during his lifetime might well form the nucleus of the first two sections of the Buddhist canon—

the sutras and the codes of conduct. After his parinirvana, the sangha spread across the Indian subcontinent, and the new monastic communities tried to organize, interpret, and consolidate his teachings. They developed a system of thought called *abhidharma*, which can be roughly translated as "higher" or "further" teachings. The early texts from this collection are considered to be a third section of the canon. Together these three collections are known as the *tripitaka*, or "three baskets" of the teachings (so called because of the way the original palm-leaf manuscripts were stored).

Initially, the abhidharma systematization involved arranging the main points of the teachings into lists of concepts. These lists served as mnemonic devices for what, at that time, was still an oral tradition. Sometimes these lists were arranged in numerical sequences—a section devoted to single things, followed by a section for pairs of things, a section for threefold things, and so on. The composers of these lists were very conservative. This is how Johannes Bronkhorst, a contemporary scholar of early Buddhism, describes the process:

> They first introduce a short sutra text, and then this text
> and the doctrines it contains are subsequently explained in
> detail. This shows how the authors of these treatises pro-
> ceeded. The words of the Buddha transmitted by tradition
> provided their basis. Nothing new was added except that
> the doctrines were arranged into lists. The Buddhists of
> that period were concerned not to add anything new to the
> teachings of the Buddha.[4]

Along with systematizing the teachings in the sutras, these

early Buddhists pursued a second approach of interpretation. They minutely examined their meditation experiences to distinguish what seemed to be fundamentally real from what was merely conventionally believed to exist. This led to what they called *dharma theory*. (The use of the term *dharma*, in this case, does not refer to the teachings, or the truth. Here, *dharma* refers to the most basic psychophysical constituents of experience.)

The dharma theory holds that our world of lasting people and places is fabricated by conceptuality out of momentary bits of experience. These moments of experience are the dharmas. People and places are merely imputed to exist based on experiencing sequences of dharmas. Only the dharmas, and their interactions, are ultimately real. The dharma theory is an atomistic model of experience that is constantly arising and disintegrating. The purpose of investigating experience in this way is not to come up with abstract theories about reality but to guide practitioners toward liberating insights. Buddhist author Noa Ronkin explains the core of abhidharma thought this way:

> The increasingly detailed enumerations of dharmas demonstrate that no essence or independent self could be found in any phenomenon or its constituents, since all aspects of experience are impermanent, arising and passing away subject to numerous causes and conditions. . . . The practice of the discrimination of dharmas thus undermines the apparently solid world we emotionally and intellectually grasp at, that is replete with objects of desire and attachment.[5]

Abhidharma texts provide methods for investigating the nature of experience that break down the reified concepts of the self and phenomena that hold samsara together. It is this style of investigation that is radically advanced by the development of the Mahayana.

13

The Mahayana Emerges

I suspect it might indeed have been quite possible to visit India in earlier classical times and as a casual visitor not see Mahayana Buddhism as such at all. I am sure that great Mahayana thinkers like Nagarjuna (c. second century C.E.) or Asanga (c. fourth century C.E.) would not have appeared much different from their non-Mahayana brethren. As Indians they would have looked, dressed and conducted themselves in a way akin to, say, a modern Theravadin in Sri Lanka. Their public behavior might not have been significantly different from that of non-Mahayanists. Perhaps even their public utterances would not have been very different. But if one came to know them well or visited them in their rooms or cells perhaps one could have detected a different vision and intention, a different idea of what, ultimately, it all meant.

—*Paul Williams*[1]

A ROUND THE SECOND or first century B.C.E., at the time the earliest teachings were being committed to writing, a new cycle of sutras began to appear called Prajnaparamita (Perfection of Wisdom). Their status as words of the Buddha was controversial, but they gradually developed a following. The Prajnaparamita sutras took the insights of the abhidharma much further. It was not just people and places that were fabricated by conceptuality. Even the dharmas lacked true nature. They proclaimed that the nature of all phenomena is *shunyata* (emptiness):

> The primary subject matter of the Prajnaparamita sutras, what they teach explicitly is the actual nature of emptiness, which is explained through various formats such as the three doors to liberation. . . . The sutras also lay out the gradual subjective process of realizing emptiness; that is, how prajna is perfected in the mind. This is why the texts always refer to "the perfection (paramita) of prajna"—they never say "the perfection of emptiness" or "the perfection of the nature of phenomena." Of course, by definition, there is nothing to be perfected in emptiness or the true nature of phenomena anyway, but there is a lot to be perfected in our awareness of this nature. Thus, prajnaparamita means perfecting not the ultimate object to be realized but the realization of this object.[2]

The Prajnaparamita sutras also present a new vision of the path to this realization. The motivation they proclaim is the *bodhisattva ideal*, and the practices they prescribe are the *paramita disciplines*: the perfections of generosity, discipline, patience, effort, meditation, and wisdom. The notion of the bodhisattva, a being who's aim is not just personal liberation but the attainment of perfect buddhahood for the benefit of all sentient beings, existed in the earliest teachings. But the Mahayana sutras took what had been a historical description of a future buddha and transformed it into an ideal motivation to which all practitioners could aspire.

The Mahayana sutras introduced many elements that are not found in the earlier sutras. They contain vast cosmologies and mythologies, stories of pure lands and cosmic buddhas and bodhisattvas. But their most important contribution was the profound view of shunyata and the powerful practices they proposed to realize that reality.

Evolution Not Revolution

For many years, scholars of Buddhism assumed that the Mahayana began as a reform movement, challenging the orthodoxy of the mainstream abhidharma schools in the same way that Protestants rebelled against the Roman Catholic Church. Recently, it's become clear that the evidence does not support the imposition of this Western historical model on the Indian Buddhist experience. The current view is that the Mahayana arose as fresh insights and practices within the existing monastic orders. Mahayanists did not set up separate schools or sects, and didn't create a separate Vinaya or ordination lineage. Mahayana monastics continued to be formal members of the early schools and continued to follow their rules of conduct. Paul Willams writes,

> We now know that a picture of schism and sect, with
> attendant and widespread rivalry and antagonism, would

be very misleading. We know from later Chinese sources, for example, that Chinese pilgrims to India found so-called non-Mahayana and Mahayana monks in the same monasteries. The only obvious and manifest differences between these two groups was that the Mahayana monks showed particular reverence, "worshipped," figures of bodhisattvas, compassionate beings on the path to full Buddhahood, while the non-Mahayana monks chose not to.[3]

Living Dharma

This sketch of early Buddhist history shows that the presentation of the buddhadharma evolved gradually after the time of the Buddha. Of course, there are people who claim that only the texts and methods of their sect are the original and true teachings of the Buddha and decry anything else as heresy. But this sectarian approach fails to recognize the living quality of the dharma.

The authority of the Buddha's teachings does not rest on the history of particular texts and methods. It rests on the realizations of those who are guided by these teachings. As the sangha and society change, the teachings need to evolve with them to continue to be effective guides for the path to liberation.

In *Cutting Through Spiritual Materialism*, Trungpa Rinpoche described the continual renewal of the dharma in this way:

Knowledge is not handed down like an antique. Rather, one teacher experiences the truth of the teachings, and he hands it down as inspiration to his student. That inspiration awakens the student, as his teacher was awakened before him. Then the student hands down the teachings to another student and so the process goes. The teachings are always up-to-date. They are not "ancient wisdom," an old legend. The teachings are not passed along as information, handed down as a grandfather tells traditional folktales to his grandchildren. It does not work that way. It is a real experience.

The teachings have the quality of warm, fresh baked bread; the bread is still warm and hot and fresh. Each baker must apply the general knowledge of how to make bread to his particular dough and oven. Then he must personally experience the freshness of this bread and must cut it fresh and eat it warm. He must make the teachings his own and then must practice them. It is a very living process.[4]

14

The Middle Way

Mahayana philosophical texts cover many of the same
topics and use many of the same methods found in
Euro-American philosophical traditions. And, as in
classical Greece, *philosophy* here must not be inter-
preted as dry theory, but rather as systematic thought
that is meant to explain, guide, and sustain contemplative practices. . . . In a fundamental way Buddhist
thinkers link their arguments to specific contemplative practices, such as meditations that analyze
personal identity. This linkage reflects the avowed
soteriological [aiming for liberation] context of all
Buddhist thought, namely, the cultivation of meditative experiences that allegedly eliminate suffering and
lead to *nirvana*. Indeed, from the traditional view, the
Buddhist thinker's philosophical work was itself a kind
of spiritual practice that moved the thinker closer to
these final goals. Philosophy is therefore called "seeing" (*darshana*), a metaphor that evokes a central goal
of Buddhist contemplative practice: an experience
(*anubhava*) in which one sees things as they truly are.

—*John Dunne*[1]

THE LITERATURE OF BUDDHISM is rich and diverse. Occasionally, it seems contradictory. The Buddha sometimes said, "I am." Sometimes he taught that there is no self. Some commentators present things from one perspective. Others present opposing things from a different perspective. As the dharma evolved, the number of perspectives multiplied, making it hard to see the underlying unity of the teachings. Over time, several interpretive schemes have attempted to reconcile these seeming paradoxes.

One approach classifies the teachings as either *provisional* or *definitive*. Teachings that are presented from the perspective of ordinary people, rather than the perspective of realized beings, are classified as provisional teachings. For example, at times the Buddha said that there is a material world, that persons exist, that the past, present, and future exist, that suffering really exists, and that enlightenment is a real thing. He laid out a path of view, meditation, and conduct to lead practitioners from bondage to liberation. These are provisional teachings, taught from the conventional perspective, in a way that we ordinary people can understand.

Other teachings are said to be definitive because they were taught from the perspective of enlightened beings, who see genuine reality just as it is. From that perspective, a material world, the self, the three times, suffering, enlightenment, and the path to liberation are all like illusions and dreams. They are all empty of any nature. Liberation already exists within us, but it is temporarily obscured by incidental stains.

A second interpretive approach divides the teachings into three groups. The *three dharmachakras*, or three turnings of the wheel of dharma, is a quasi-historical presentation of the evolution of the teachings. In this traditional way of presenting things, it is said that the Buddha set the wheel of the dharma in motion three times.

First, he taught the four truths and the eightfold path, from the conventional perspective, to people who were seeking their own liberation. They believed in their own reality and the reality of their suffering. To help them overcome the delusion of clinging to a self, he taught the four marks: that impermanence, suffering, and selflessness really exist, and that only nirvana is peace.

As the sangha expanded and matured, and many of the Buddha's followers had loosened the grip of clinging to a self, he presented a more profound cycle of teachings: the Prajnaparamita sutras that emphasize shunyata, the practice of the paramitas, and the bodhisattva ideal. This was the second turning of the wheel of dharma.

Somewhat later, the Buddha presented a further cycle of teachings: what became known as Yogachara and the Tathagatagarbha sutras, or the sutras on buddha nature. These teachings explain that genuine reality is not simply emptiness or phenomena's lack of nature, but the inseparability of samsara and nirvana: confusion and wisdom are two different ways of experiencing the same reality. This was the third turning of the wheel of dharma.

Buddhist scholars disagree about which teachings are provisional and which are definitive, about which teachings are the actual words of the Buddha and which were composed long after he passed into nirvana, about which of the three turnings reflect the final intention of the Buddha, and so on. Well, that is what scholars do. There's a nice Tibetan saying about that: "If two yogis disagree, one of them is not a yogi. If two scholars *agree*, one of them is not a scholar."

Noble Nagarjuna

Very little is known about the life of Nagarjuna, except that he was a Buddhist monk who probably lived in southern India around the first or second century C.E. What we do know is that he profoundly influenced the development of the buddhadharma. After the Buddha himself, Nagarjuna is widely considered to be the most significant teacher in the Mahayana tradition.

It's uncertain exactly which texts Nagarjuna composed, but writings generally attributed to him are sometimes classified into three collections, which accord with the three turnings of the wheel of dharma. The *Collection of Advice* explains how virtue and nonvirtue lead to nirvana and samsara respectively, which is the approach of the first-turning teachings. The *Collection of Reasoning* focuses on shunyata and clarifies the meaning of the Prajnaparamita sutras from the middle turning. The *Collection of Praises* concerns wisdom and buddha nature, which is related to the third-turning teachings.

Nagarjuna's most important work is the *Fundamental Wisdom of the Middle Way*, or in its Sanskrit title, the *Mulamadhyamaka-karika*, which belongs to the *Collection of Reasoning*. Originally, this work was probably titled simply *Prajna* (wisdom). The focus of this treatise is emptiness. Nagarjuna's approach to teaching emptiness later became known as Madhyamaka, or the Middle Way.

In the sutras, the term *middle way* was originally used by the Buddha when he first taught the dharma to his former companions at the Deer Park in Sarnath. At that time, he used it to describe the eightfold path as a middle way between indulgence and asceticism. In later teachings, he used the term to describe a view that is a middle way between the extremes of eternalism and nihilism. In Nagarjuna's case, middle way means not falling into views of existence and nonexistence.

The *Fundamental Wisdom of the Middle Way* consists of twenty-seven chapters that use logical reasoning to examine all the phenomena of samsara and nirvana. The verses are terse and difficult to understand without a commentary. It is also easy to be misled by the seemingly intellectual nature of Nagarjuna's method.

Unlike the usual use of logic to prove an abstract conclusion, Nagarjuna does not use logic to prove anything. He does not try to prove that phenomena are empty, nor any other thesis, since such a conclusion would be within the realm of the conceptual mind, and it is the conceptual mind that obscures the liberating wisdom that realizes shunyata. Nagarjuna's goal is to reveal shunyata to us directly. He uses logical tools to short-circuit the conceptual mind, to uncover the wisdom that lies beyond the intellect. He does this using logic that exposes the absurdities of our beliefs about the phenomena we experience.

The things that we experience—trees, houses, friends, enemies—seem to exist in just the way they appear to us. They all seem to have histories and futures. They all seem to have been produced. They seem to come and go. That maple tree in the garden was once just a seedling. It was planted years ago, and now it towers over the house. If you look at that tree now, and look again tomorrow, it will still be there—the same tree. It must really exist!

That's the way things seem to us as ordinary people. However, for beings who have realized the true nature of reality, each and every thing that appears depends on its specific causes and conditions, while being empty of any nature of its own. Things do not come from anywhere and they do not go anywhere. They do not last; neither are they nonexistent. Whatever appears to us is merely a dependently arisen appearance, free from all our projections about what it could be. As the great Tibetan yogi Milarepa sang, "The phenomena of the three realms of samsara; while not existing, they appear—how incredibly amazing!"

Dependent arising is often confused with the popular notion of interdependence or interconnectedness—that nothing exists all on its own; all things are influenced by other things; we are all connected to each other. For example, it is sometimes said that when a butterfly beats its wings in the Amazon, that affects the weather in North America. Interdependence is presented from the conventional perspective that all these things exist.

When Nagarjuna uses dependent arising, the meaning is qualitatively different. In the teachings of the Middle Way, dependent arising is synonymous with emptiness. Whatever depends on causes and conditions for its appearance is empty of an essence. It is a dependently arisen mere appearance. Emptiness does not mean nonexistence. It means freedom from conceptual fabrications: empty while appearing, appearing while being empty.

To understand dependent arising, it helps to remember that the past is gone—it no longer exists. The future has not arisen—it does not yet exist. We can only experience present appearances. Everything else is mentally fabricated by the conceptual mind.

15

Experiencing Emptiness

> Nagarjuna's approach is similar to having an execu-
> tioner order his or her own execution.
>
> —*The Ninth Karmapa, Wangchuk Dorje*[1]

IF YOU APPROACH them with inquisitiveness, the contemplations in the *Fundamental Wisdom of the Middle Way* can cut
through your conceptual fabrications and bring about direct
experiences of shunyata. They take some effort to grapple with,
but it is well worth it. Here are a few key selections from the text
for you to play with.

The first chapter is an examination of causality. The purpose
of this chapter is to challenge our assumptions that things really
exist because they've been produced by real causes and conditions, which also really exist.

Nagarjuna begins his assault in this way:

Not from self, not from other,
Not from both, nor without cause:

Things do not arise
At any place, at any time.[2]

How is it possible that things do not arise? It seems like things are produced all the time. In this verse, Nagarjuna identifies the four possible relations that causes and effects might have. Logically, if there are truly existing results, they must have one of these relationships to their causes:

1. The result already exists within its causes (arising from self)
2. The result does not exist within its causes, but comes into existence because of them (arising from other)
3. Some combination of 1 and 2 produce a truly existing result (arising from both self and other)
4. A truly existing result arises without any causes

I encourage you to do this investigation yourself. It's quite challenging because it directly contradicts the way we normally think about things. That can be very irritating. But if you persist with this inquiry, it will spark insight.

I will go through each possibility in turn; then please try to apply these reasonings to your own examples.

1. The result already exists within its causes

If things arose from themselves, that is, if the result already existed within its causes, to say that it arose would be meaningless, since arising means something coming into existence anew. How could something that already exists come into existence? Another absurd consequence of things arising from themselves is that they would always be arising. Since their causes would always be present, they could not stop arising!

2. The result does not exist within its causes but comes into existence because of them

If things don't arise from themselves—if results are truly different things from causes—how could the result get its nature from its causes? They are unrelated things, like a dog and a cat. Another absurd consequence of things arising from causes that are different from themselves is that they would arise from what is not their causes as well as things that are their causes because causes and noncauses equally lack connection with the result. If this were true, they could arise from anything at all.

3. The result arises from both itself and causes other than itself

Since each of the first two positions are not logically tenable, you might think combining them might somehow remedy the situation, but this only compounds the problem. Asserting that things arise from both themselves and causes other than themselves is a logical contradiction. It inherits the faults of both positions.

4. A truly existing result arises without any causes

Finally, if things don't arise from themselves or something other than themselves, maybe things arise without cause. But if that were the case, things would either always be present or never be present. They would always be present because they don't need causes to arise, or they would never be present because even if their causes did come together they could not produce anything. Either you would not need to do anything to accomplish whatever you want, or whatever you did wouldn't produce any results.

This is one set of reasonings. A few verses later, Nagarjuna gives another set, asking: Do results exist at the time of their causes or not? If results already exist at the time of their causes, what role do the causes play? The results already exist! If the results do not exist at the time of their causes, what role do the causes play? How could causes have any connection with results that do not yet exist?

Doing the Investigation

A classical illustration of this investigation is the relationship of fire and fuel. Fire—the result—appears when its causes—fuel, an ignition source, and a suitable atmosphere—come together.

If fire already existed within its causes, fuel would be hot and burning without any fire. You would be able to cook a meal over fuel even when it wasn't ignited! If fire and fuel were different inherently existing things, fire could equally arise from anything—fuel, water, or steel beams. Fire cannot be both the same as fuel and different from fuel. Finally, fire does not spontaneously appear without any causes.

Another classical example is the relationship of sprouts to seeds. Someone might think that the sprout already exists, in some fashion, within the seed, but if the sprout already exists, there would be no need to bring the seed, soil, moisture, and warmth together to grow a plant. If the sprout does not exist at the time of the seed, germinating the seed in the soil with moisture and warmth would have no ability to affect the sprout since the sprout does not yet exist!

You might find it helpful to contemplate an example that is closer to home. Think of your phone and the process of producing it. It seems obvious that the phone has a history. You could imagine that the arising of the phone begins with extracting and refining oil, silicone, aluminum, and rare earth elements. These substances would be further processed into more specialized materials. These materials would be fabricated into components. Software would be conceived, written, and tested. The components and the software would be assembled into the finished device. Before the final assembly, no phone would exist. You couldn't make calls, send texts, or run apps with anything that went into the phone. At the moment the phone appears, all the activities of producing the phone no longer exist. At that point you can imagine something that seems like the production process, but the process of producing that phone can no longer be found. The phone's appearance depends on these causes—it is dependently arisen—but it is empty of them. The phone is a dependently arisen mere appearance. Each moment of the phone's production was also a dependently arisen mere appearance.

As long as we cling to the reality of things, these reasonings will seem ridiculous. We are convinced that things are real, therefore they must have an inherent nature. But these reasonings show the absurd consequences of these beliefs.

Coming and Going

The second chapter of the *Fundamental Wisdom of the Middle Way* is an examination of coming and going. This might be easier to visualize than the examination of cause and effect. Nagarjuna composed this chapter in response to our belief that things truly exist because we see them come and go.

The chapter begins with this verse:

> On the path that has been traveled, there is no moving,
> On the path that has not been traveled, there is no moving, either,
> And in some other place besides the path that has been traveled and the path that has not,
> Motions are not perceptible in any way at all.[3]

Nagarjuna's argument is that we cannot find coming or going because, when we look precisely, they are not found in any of the three times: past, present, or future. You could contemplate this claim by thinking of a car moving along a highway. It seems like we see the movement of the car along the road, but if we distinguish what we see and what appears in our mind's eye, that's not really the case. You can't see any motion of the car on the section of the road that's already been traversed. You also can't see any motion on the section of the road that the car hasn't yet passed. In between these two, it does seem like we can see the car moving—the wheels appear to spin and the car does appear to travel forward—but this apparent motion still depends on joining past, present, and future instants of perception. This is a mere appearance of motion. The key point is that you can't see the car come from one place and go to another. It seems like that is happening but only because you've included your mental images of the past and future trajectories with the mere appearance of motion in the present.

Another way to investigate this is with an example that Nagarjuna might have used: the motion of a bird flying across the sky. The bird seems to move, but you don't find any imprints in the sky of its coming or going.

The Self

The eighteenth chapter of the *Fundamental Wisdom of the Middle Way* is an examination of the self and phenomena. This, in effect, is an examination of the whole of reality. For this reason, it's considered to be the heart of the text. Earlier, we investigated selflessness and the illusion of a self. Since recognizing selflessness is essential to realizing freedom, I encourage you to explore this again, this time using Nagarjuna's reasonings.

The eighteenth chapter begins with this verse:

> If the self were the aggregates,
> It would be something that arises and ceases.
> If the self were something other than the aggregates,
> It would not have the aggregates' characteristics.[4]

A translation of the Sanskrit term *skandha* is "aggregate." Other translations are "collection," "heap," or—one I really like—the "disintegrating collection." This last one conveys the dynamic, constantly changing quality of the skandhas. Five skandhas are enumerated and described: the skandhas of forms, feelings, discriminations, mental formations, and consciousnesses. In detail they are:

- The *skandha of forms* includes the experiences of the five sense faculties and their objects. It consists of all the experiences that we think of as the material world.

- The *skandha of feelings* consists of all pleasant, unpleasant, and indifferent sensations.
- The *skandha of discriminations* includes all experiences of characteristics, qualities, or distinguishing features.
- The *skandha of mental formations* includes all the thoughts, emotions, and mental states that are not included in the other four skandhas.
- The *skandha of consciousnesses* includes the clear, knowing aspect of each sensory and mental experience.

The skandhas are continually arising and ceasing. Your experience is constantly changing. One moment you experience a sight, the next moment a feeling, the next a thought, then a tactile sensation; each one replacing the one that came before. Despite the transience of experience, the world seems solid and enduring because there seems to be a solid, lasting self in the middle of all this change.

Nagarjuna reasons that if this self were the same as these disintegrating collections, it wouldn't be what we imagine the self to be: a stable experiencer of phenomena. There is no stability in the skandhas. Also, if the self were the same as the skandhas, there would be many selves, just as the skandhas are multiplicities.

If the self were something different from the skandhas, it would not have any qualities at all since everything with qualities is already included in the five skandhas. Contemplate this for yourself. Can you find a stable, lasting experiencer that is not just a constantly changing collection of forms, feelings, discriminations, mental formations, or consciousnesses? What could such a self be like?

The next verse presents the logical consequences of not finding a self that is either the same as the skandhas or different from them:

If there is no "me" in the first place,
How could there be anything that belongs to me?
When "me" and "mine" are found to be peace,
Clinging to "me" and "mine" ceases.[5]

When we see that the self is an illusion and that objects are just dependently arisen appearances, we experience genuine reality, just as it is. When we see that, it is as Suzuki Roshi described: "Everything is just flashing into the vast phenomenal world."[6]

Breaking the Chains

Subsequent chapters of the *Fundamental Wisdom of the Middle Way* examine actors and actions, samsara, suffering, contact, karma, time, the Buddha, mistakes, nirvana—the complete range of entities that early Buddhists thought truly existed, using similar reasonings to the ones we have just looked at.

After struggling with these reasonings for a while, you might decide that this is just a bunch of philosophical nonsense. You might think that these teachings are only for pointy-headed intellectuals and dharma nerds. You might be tempted to put down this book and walk away. But there are good reasons to stick with it. By repeatedly going through this type of investigation, you could glimpse the emptiness of phenomena. By experiencing emptiness again and again, the habit of taking things to be truly real will weaken. This is liberating.

When we don't recognize that phenomena are empty of our projections, appearances trigger reactions that are causes of suffering. The moment we see something or hear something, rather than appreciating it as appearance-emptiness, we start thinking something. A whole background for that sight or sound proliferates in our minds so quickly that we don't even know that it's happening. We imagine the past and the future and take an emotional stance. Thoughts proliferate and we are driven to act. We get bound up in these chain reactions without even knowing what has happened.

When you spot a pile of dirty dishes in the sink, you don't see them as dependently arisen appearances, free from past and future, coming and going. In an instant, an image of the probable perpetrator arises in your mind. That mental image seems to be part of the perception of the mess itself. Your partner/child/parent/housemate has been inconsiderate, leaving another mess for you to clean up. Irritation arises. You think about what to say, how to get them to clean up after themselves, and so on. When you do recognize that appearances are empty, the chain reactions are cut. You can still understand the dependent nature of the appearances, but you are no longer helplessly caught up in your own reactivity.

16

Two Realities

Since all things can be seen genuinely or falsely,
Every thing bears two natures.
The Buddha taught that the object of genuine seeing is
   suchness
And that false seeing is the relative truth.

—*Chandrakirti*[1]

I HAVE A CALLIGRAPHY in my living room that was painted by my teacher Chögyam Trungpa Rinpoche. It's a Tibetan transliteration of the Sanskrit word *mudra*, which means "symbol" or "gesture." The calligraphy was a gift from Rinpoche that was sent to me when I was living in Paris with my family in the 1980s.

Strictly speaking, none of this is true. The calligraphy that I now see has no relationship to the one I remember receiving. It is empty of all my fabrications about what it is: its past, its present, or its future. Ultimately, the nature of this fresh moment of experience is emptiness. Conventionally—the way we normally think about things—the story of the calligraphy is accurate.

We experience two realities: the reality of dependently arisen appearances and the reality of our thoughts. To the deluded mind, these seem to all be one reality. When I look at the calligraphy, it seems to *really be* the word *mudra*, to *be* a gift from Trungpa Rinpoche. I don't distinguish what *I see* from my *conceptions about it*. These fabrications seem to exist objectively, right within the object. In fact, they only exist subjectively, within the mind of the subject.

If someone else walks into the room, someone who can't read Tibetan, who doesn't know who painted the calligraphy or how it came to be there, they would have a completely different experience. They would experience similar visual appearances but completely different thoughts about what they were viewing.

These two ways of experiencing are called *samvriti satya* and *paramartha satya* in Sanskrit, terms that are often translated into English as relative truth and ultimate truth.

Satya means "reality or truth." *Samvriti* means "conventional or relative," but it also has the connotation of concealing, obscuring, or deceiving. Samvriti satya is conventional reality—truth, or reality, that conceals. Normally, we think of truth as something that reveals, but samvriti satya is truth that both reveals and conceals. What it reveals is our understanding of what things are, why things happen, how things fit into the world. What it conceals is the nature of our experience.

Paramartha means "highest, supreme, or absolute." Absolute reality is what is directly perceived by prajnaparamita or wisdom. Followers of the Middle Way describe this reality as shunyata (emptiness). It is not nothingness but rather the dynamic display of emptiness: dependently arisen sights, sounds, tastes, smells, tactile sensations, and mental phenomena that appear, while having no nature of their own.

To get a feel for these two realities, think of someone you know. When you do this, they will seem to exist in certain ways: having a certain temperament, a certain history, certain ways of behaving. You will also have attitudes toward this person. When you talk with your friends, they might have similar feelings and narratives. You might also know people with very different concepts about that person. That person will have still another very different picture of themselves. All these versions of the person are merely conventionally real. They seem to be what the person actually is, but ultimately, the person is free from all these fabrications—even their own. The nature of that person is emptiness. Relative reality conceals what is ultimately real.

The Conventional

Conventional reality only appears to the conceptual mind. It does not appear to the senses. The brilliant twentieth-century Tibetan scholar Gendun Chöpel explained it in this way:

> All of our decisions about what is and is not are just decisions made in accordance with how it appears to our mind; they have no other basis whatsoever. Therefore, when we ask, "Does it exist or not?" and the other person answers, "It exists," in fact, we are asking, "Does this appear to your mind to exist or not exist?" and the answer is simply, "It appears to my mind to exist." In the same way, everything that one asks about—better or worse, good or bad, beautiful or ugly—is in fact merely asked about for the sake of understanding how the other person thinks. That the other person makes a decision and answers is in fact just a decision made

in accordance with how it appears to his or her own mind; there is no other reason whatsoever. Therefore, as long as the ideas of two people are in disagreement with each other, they will argue. When they agree, the very thing that they agree upon will be placed in the class of what is, what exists, what can be known, and what is valid, and so on. Thus, the more people there are who agree, the more the point they agree upon becomes of great significance and importance. Contrary views are taken to be wrong views, mistaken perceptions, and so on. . . .[2]

And:

But is it not appropriate to place one's confidence in that very decision which has been made by one's own mind? It is not the case. Sometimes this mind of ours seems mistaken, sometimes it seems correct. It is established by experience that it is always deceptive, like the divination of a bad soothsayer. Who can trust it? Many things that are decided to be in the morning are decided not to be in the evening. Things that are decided to be early in life are decided not to be later in life. Things that one hundred thousand Muslims decide are true are decided to be false by one hundred thousand Buddhists.[3]

You may well resist this way of understanding reality. After all, we learn from an early age that the world exists independently of our thoughts. There are facts about this world and statements about these facts that are either true or false. It's natural to think that relative truth must be grounded in the way things really are.

But if these truths are not part of the fabric of reality, what are they?

Conventional reality is based on the common consensus of humans. Take money, for example. Those pieces of paper that we call currency, the balances in our bank accounts, the payments we send and receive, all seem meaningful and very, very real. We can exchange them for tangible goods and services of all kinds. Money can even be a matter of life or death. Yet, there is nothing in those dollars, euros, and pesos that gives them any reality other than our shared conceptions of their value. This is not difficult to understand. We see this quite vividly when people lose faith in a currency because of hyper-inflation causing the value to disappear.

Measurements of time are also conventional reality. The days of the week, the hours of the day, the months of the year—all these are merely conceptions. They work as long as we all agree to them. They are just fabrications, but they are useful fabrications. If you agree to meet your friends at 2:00 p.m. on Tuesday, you and your friends can bring about the causes and conditions for that meeting to take place.

The shapes of the letters on this page, the sounds they signify, the meanings of these words—all these are merely conventions that have been drilled into you so thoroughly that when you look at these shapes, the sounds and meanings actually seem to exist on the page. But the sounds and meanings have no existence beyond your own mind.

Some conventional realities are merely dependently imputed. Fast depends on slow. Large depends on small. Beautiful depends on ugly. None of these exist apart from the conceptions.

Some conventional truths are derived from observing patterns of dependent arising. Farmers see that the appearance of strong, healthy plants depends on gathering certain conditions of soil, seeds, water, and weather. Concepts about these dependencies are shared with other farmers, and they become the common consensus about farming.

Scientific Realities

The realities established by science and technology might seem to be of an entirely different order. They might seem ultimately true; proven by the amazing things that these methods are able to predict and produce. However, even these realities are merely conventional. The scientific method consists of clearly articulated procedures for observation and theory formation that produce rigorous conceptual models of reality, but these models are not genuine reality itself. They are mental constructions: abstractions of reality.

In his Herbert Spencer Lecture, delivered at Oxford in 1933, Albert Einstein described the relationship between scientific theory and direct experience:

I want now to glance for a moment at the development of the theoretical method, and while doing so especially to observe the relation of pure theory to the totality of the data of experience. Here is the eternal antithesis of the two inseparable constituents of human knowledge, Experience and Reason, within the sphere of physics. We honour ancient Greece as the cradle of western science. She for the first time created the intellectual miracle of a logical system, the assertions of which followed one from another with such rigor that not one of the demonstrated propositions admitted of the slightest doubt—Euclid's geometry. . . . But yet the time was not ripe for a science that could comprehend reality, was not ripe until a second elementary truth had been realized, which only became the common property of philosophers after Kepler and Galileo. Pure logical thinking can give us no knowledge whatsoever of the world of experience; all knowledge about reality begins with experience and terminates in it.

Conclusions obtained by purely rational processes are, so far as Reality is concerned, entirely empty.[4]

The great Danish physicist Niels Bohr wrote this about the relationship of physics to experience: "Physics is to be regarded not so much as the study of something *a priori* given, but as the development of methods for ordering and surveying human experience."[5]

Science functions. It is useful. It can reveal profound and subtle things about the dependent appearances of this world. Science also conceals. When we think about the world in physical, chemical, or biological terms, whether at the elementary school level or the postdoctoral level, that thinking conceals the dynamic display of empty appearance. We don't recognize the nature of the conceptuality that appears to our minds. We take the abstractions to be real stuff, and these beliefs confirm our impressions that the world consists of solid, lasting, independently existing things, and that we are also solid, lasting, independently existing things. We are bound by these conceptions, and all the conditioning that arises from them, and thus fail to realize the peace that lies beyond conceptions.

17

Illusory Forms

Everything is neither true nor false.
Everything resembles water-moons.

—*Two-Part Hevajra Tantra*[1]

To bring these teachings to life, try to reflect on the way they apply to your ordinary experience. When you have confidence in your understanding, then bring that understanding into your meditation practice. Here are a few contemplations to get you started.

Vignette One

You watch a movie with some friends. Afterward, some of them say they liked the film, some say they didn't like it, and some say that it was just okay. Did you all see the same movie?

Each of you probably saw roughly the same patterns of light projected on the screen and heard roughly the same sounds coming from the speakers. What was different for each of you was what arose in your minds as you watched the movie. The images that you experienced as "people" and "places" were mental images. They were projections that arose in your minds. Movies are fantastic methods for creating these illusions. There were no real people or places on the screen, just patterns of light. Each of you had a distinctly different experience, even though you all claimed to have seen the same movie. No wonder you had different feelings about what you saw. Only part of the movie that you experienced existed on the screen. However, you can't say that the movie didn't exist. Each of you experienced a vivid display of sights, sounds, and mind.

Vignette Two

In the morning you practice meditation at home. Taking a good posture, you apply yourself to the technique. Soon, you are engaged in grappling with a family problem. The other family members almost seem to be present in the room as you go back and forth with various arguments. After a while you notice you are distracted and return to applying the technique. Soon, you are thinking about what you need to do after you finish practicing. It's almost as if you are already engaged in that activity. When you notice the distraction, you come back. Soon, a TV show you watched the previous evening comes to mind, and you comment to yourself about the characters; then you come back.

Even though you don't move from the spot where you are sitting, a variety of situations arise as powerful presences in your mind, and then they dissipate. It seems like they are all "out there," just waiting for you to shift your attention to them. But there is really nothing out there, besides the spaciousness of your mind manifesting as these various situations.

Vignette Three

You hear a dog barking . . . and then you remember. You can't hear a dog; you hear a sound. You see your face in the mirror . . . and then you remember; you can't see your own face. You see a reflection. You smell dinner . . . and then you remember; you can't smell dinner. You smell an aroma.

Vignette Four

Your mother is talking to you in a familiar way, but there are other people popping in and out of the room, and you're not sure you understand what is going on. You would like to ask your mother about this, but suddenly things get emotional, and you're not sure what to do.

And then you wake up.

Everyday Practice

We are surrounded by mirages. The reality of what we see, hear, feel, and so on is continually intermingled with projected realities. We believe that our projections really exist in the way we experience them. When we see that they are actually movements of our own minds, we begin to overcome the delusions of these appearances.

A water-moon is a classical illustration of illusion. Standing by a lake on a cloud-free night, when the moon has risen and the water is not roiled by wind, you might see the moon reflected in the water. Of course, there is no moon in the water! But when the appropriate causes and conditions gather, it appears to be there. There are other traditional examples such as optical illusions, dreams, echoes, mirages, and magic spells. They appear to be one thing, but actually they are not that thing at all. This is not difficult to understand, but the illusory nature of daily experience is much more elusive.

Once you have some understanding of the way ordinary reality is deceptive, there is an excellent practice to help turn that understanding into direct experience. This practice is known by various names: the samadhi of illusion, the practice of illusory form, the practice of pure perception. Khenpo Tsültrim Gyamtso Rinpoche describes the practice this way:

> View all appearances of forms, sounds, smells, tastes, tactile
> sensations, and thoughts as appearing while empty, empty
> while appearing; understand all your experiences to be
> the union of appearance and emptiness, like illusions and
> dreams.
>
> These days, the samadhi that sees everything to be like
> an illusion is easier to practice than ever before, because
> modern technology has produced so many new examples of
> empty forms. Movies, television, telephones, fax, e-mail, the
> internet—all of these are wonderful examples of how things
> can appear due to the coming together of causes and conditions while at the same time being empty of any inherent
> nature. In big cities, there are all kinds of flashing lights and
> moving billboards on the outside, and when you go into any
> big department store, there are huge mirrors on the walls,

filled with reflected images. So the city is a wonderful place to train in the samadhi of illusion.[2]

When you do this practice, you quickly notice how everyone and everything gets labeled and described. It happens so quickly that you usually don't notice that these labels and descriptions get superimposed on space: the pure appearances of empty sights, sounds, and tastes.

18

Two Brothers Take It to Another Level

The experience of complete freedom from conceptual contrivance must also be the experience of the clear light nature of mind. . . . [A follower of the Middle Way] who denies this must still have some subtle concept which is obscuring or negating this reality; in other words, he has not truly realized complete freedom from conceptual contrivance. This happens because for a long time the meditator has been cutting through illusion and seeing emptiness as a kind of negation. This becomes such a strong habit that even when the experience of absolute reality, the clear light nature of mind, starts to break through like the sun from behind clouds, the meditator automatically turns his mind toward it to subtly negate it. . . . [Yogacarins] argue that if there really were no conceptual contrivance in the mind, the clear light nature would shine forth so clearly and unmistakably that it would not be possible to deny it.

—*Khenpo Tsültrim Gyamtso Rinpoche*[1]

YOU NEED A SENSE OF HUMOR to progress along the Buddhist path because the remedies to delusion often become new obstacles. For example, you might contemplate Nagarjuna's investigations and experience glimpses of shunyata, the remedies to the mirage of ego-clinging. What happens next? You take pride in that experience: "I experienced emptiness. I experienced selflessness. This is shunyata!"

Ego uses the very thread of insight to reweave its illusory cocoon. This doesn't completely negate the insight. The solid conception of a self will still be undermined. However, ego's tendency to use insights to reinforce itself is an obstacle: it's two steps forward and another step back. This is typical of the way delusion perpetuates itself and one of the things that makes the journey to liberation long and challenging. You can't completely dissolve delusion with a single profound insight. It's wash, rinse, repeat—all the way down.

The way the Buddhist teachings evolved follows much the same pattern. The dharma theory of the Abhidharmikas is a powerful method for cutting through clinging to the self, but clinging to the real existence of dharmas becomes an obstacle to recognizing the true nature of phenomena. The Madhyamaka reasonings that reveal phenomenal emptiness are remedies for clinging to the true existence of dharmas, but clinging to the emptiness of phenomena becomes an obstacle to recognizing the true nature of the mind.

Nagarjuna's methods rip holes in the fabric of conceptuality and directly reveal the inexpressible nature of phenomena. But these experiences are not things we can hold on to. He made it clear that even concepts of emptiness must be abandoned. The seventh verse of chapter thirteen of the *Fundamental Wisdom of the Middle Way* states:

If there were the slightest thing not empty,
There would be that much emptiness existent.
Since, however, there is not the slightest thing not empty,
How could emptiness exist?[2]

It is only when you abandon clinging to concepts of existence
and nonexistence that the inexpressible is revealed. This experience is perfect and utter peace, as the eighth verse of chapter five
describes:

Those with little intelligence
View things as being existent or nonexistent.
They do not see that what is to be seen
Is perfect and utter peace.[3]

But questions remain. If all phenomena are ultimately free of
fabrications and their nature is perfect and utter peace, how does
delusion arise? How does traveling the path transform suffering
into freedom? On a practical level, how do followers of the Middle Way cultivate the experience of emptiness without falling into
nihilism?

Asanga

Roughly two centuries after Nagarjuna, two half brothers developed an approach that addressed these issues. Asanga, the older
brother, was born during the fourth century c.e., in the ancient
kingdom of Gandhara. He became a monk in one of the early
Buddhist schools, and later made a powerful connection with
the Mahayana teachings. Asanga spent many years intensively

studying and practicing to realize the truth of these teachings. According to traditional accounts, he spent twelve years meditating in solitary retreats before finally meeting the great bodhisattva Maitreya, the future buddha, face-to-face.

You might wonder if these traditional accounts mean that celestial buddhas and deities really exist somewhere. That would contradict the fundamental Mahayana tenet that no phenomena truly exist. To appreciate Asanga's meeting with Maitreya, you need to know what Mahayanists mean when they speak of buddhas and deities. Sometimes, buddhas and deities are used symbolically. They are modeled after things we are familiar with—like humans or animals—that possess arms and legs and heads. These anthropomorphic forms are used to point out aspects of our own minds. For example, images of five buddhas are sometimes used to indicate the true nature of the negative emotions. Vairochana represents the true nature of ignorance—all-accommodating wisdom; Akshobhya represents the true nature of anger—mirrorlike wisdom; Ratnasambhava represents the true nature of pride—the wisdom of equanimity; Amitabha represents the true nature of desire—discriminating wisdom; and Amoghasiddhi represents the true nature of envy—all-accomplishing wisdom.

At other times, Mahayanists use these terms to indicate the *actual* buddhas and deities. When Asanga met Maitreya, he did not meet a celestial buddha with a face and arms. He met the actual Buddha: the true nature of mind itself.

Vasubandhu

Asanga's younger brother, Vasubandhu, joined another early Buddhist school. As a young monk, he traveled to Kashmir to study abhidharma at what was then the foremost center of the Vaibhashika school, one of the main abhidharma philosophical schools. After returning to Gandhara, he taught the system he had learned in Kashmir and composed the *Treasury of the Abhidharma*, or *Abhidharmakosha*, which sets out the views of the Vaibhashika school in verse form. He also wrote an auto-commentary to his text that criticized many of the points in the Vaibhashika system from the perspective of the rival abhidharma philosophical school, the Sautrantrika.

When he was an Abhidharmika, it seems that Vasubandhu was hostile to the Mahayana until Asanga sent his students to convince him of its merits and convert him to the Mahayana. Thereafter, Vasubandhu became a powerful proponent and interpreter of the system that Asanga was developing, composing many of its core texts and commentaries.

Standing on Nagarjuna's Shoulders

Asanga and Vasubandhu did not reject earlier Mahayana teachings. They continued the development of the Mahayana on the basis of Nagarjuna's insights. There is no evidence that they saw themselves as founders of a different school, but later on, their approach was considered to be the basis for what was to be called the Yogachara tradition. This relationship is described by Richard King:

> The idea that the early classical Yogacara of Asanga and Vasubandhu found any difficulty whatsoever in embracing the basic insights of the Madhyamaka school disregards both the historical and textual evidence, which, on the

contrary, displays a spirit of underlying continuity and acceptance.

Both the Madhyamaka and the Yogacara schools accept the validity of the notions of . . . [dependent origination, selflessness of persons, selflessness of phenomena, the four truths], the bodhisattva ideal, and shunyata, among many others. With such a level of doctrinal unanimity, the two schools can hardly be said to be in great conflict with one another. Admittedly both Asanga and Vasubandhu criticize those . . . [madhyamikas who cling to nonexistence] but this is only in their attempts to delineate the true nature of emptiness as the Middle Path between extremes.[4]

19

Mere-Cognizance

For Vasubandhu the lack of a self-nature (svabhava)
just is, precisely, what he means by "appearance-
only." This is also contrary to a common understanding of Yogacara which arises from the equation of
"appearance-only" with "mind-only." This equation is
not, technically, a mistake in the case of Vasubandhu.
He says, specifically, that "mind" (citta) and "appearance" (vijnapti) are synonyms. The mistake is what
we moderns tend to think, based on a background
assumption of mind/matter Cartesian dualism—
namely, that the expression "mind only" is used to
affirm the reality of the mental at the expense of the
physical. Here, reality is certainly not physical, but
that is not Vasubandhu's point. His point is to equate
the lack of independent nature (svabhava) with the
product of mental construction. This is a simple statement of idealism, as mentioned above: Everything
that exists must either have independent existence, or
be dependent upon mind, a mental construction; and
since, for the Great Vehicle, nothing has independent
existence, everything is only a mental construction.

What it means to be "mind only," then, is not simply to
be made of mental stuff rather than physical stuff. It is
to be a false construction by a deluded mind.

—*Jonathan Gold*[1]

T HE FOUNDATION OF Asanga and Vasubandhu's system is
the insight that they called *vijnaptimatra*. There are quite a few
different English translations of this Sanskrit term, among them
"mere-cognizance," "mere-appearance," "mere-representation,"
and "mere-mental image." What the term points to is this: whatever you encounter is merely an experience of your own mind. It
is not possible to experience anything that is outside of the mind.
(Does this sound familiar?)

Asanga and Vasubandhu make it clear that the principle of
mere-cognizance is *not* the Western idealist thesis that only the
mind ultimately exists (although some of their later followers, as
well as opponents who grouped themselves under the Madhyamaka banner, argued that this is exactly what they were up to).

Common sense tells us that there is a solid world that always
exists beyond our minds; that our perceptions faithfully reveal
the world as it really is. When you look down at your hand, you
expect to see it *because it is already there*. But what if the image of
your hand is being created each time you experience it?

The commonsense rejoinder to this idea is that if I mentally
create whatever I experience, I should be able to mentally create whatever I want! How about creating a billion dollars in my
bank account? The error with this reasoning is that it assumes

we control what appears in our minds. Can you choose what thoughts you think? Can you choose what emotions you experience? Why should you be able to choose what "external" objects appear?

The principle of mere-cognizance invites you to undertake a detailed inventory of the entire range of your experience, to see if you can find some objective reality beyond the appearances in your mind. When you look at your experience of the world—beyond just sights, sounds, and mental images—what do you find? What is this world? When you look at the experience of being human—beyond just thoughts, feelings, emotions, and mental images—what do you find? What is a person?

Twenty Verses

Vasubandhu's *Twenty Verses*[2] is a text that concisely presents the view of vijnaptimatra. It will serve as a good framework for contemplating the arguments for this view. Vasubandhu presents his thesis in the first verse:

> This world is mere-cognizance,
> Since it manifests as unreal objects.
> One sees unreal objects just like people with eye disorders,
> Who see nets of hairs on the moon, and so on.[3]

There are two key points in this verse: there is something that really is experienced, and this appearance seems to be something it is not—the perceived object is unreal. The example is the hairs that you might see if you have a certain eye disease. Another classical example of an unreal object is what's traditionally referred to as a rope-snake. At twilight, in the garden, you see a piece of rope that appears to be a snake. In both of these cases, what you experience is something that objectively isn't there. Vasubandhu's point is that we continually experience mere-cognizance, and we mistake it to be the experience of real, enduring objects. These objects are unreal.

In the second verse, an opponent raises objections to this thesis:

> If an appearance does not come from an external object
> It would not be restricted to a certain time and place,
> It would not appear in many mind-streams
> And it would not be able to perform functions.[4]

Vasubandhu addresses these objections in verses three and four:

> Just as in dreams,
> Appearances are restricted to a certain time and place,
> And hungry ghosts
> All see rivers filled with pus, and so on.
>
> Images can perform functions, just as with wet-dreams.[5]

In dreams we experience appearances. While we are dreaming, they seem to be images of real objects. Everyone agrees that these dream images are not material, external objects. Asanga and Vasubandhu use dream appearances as a primary exhibit for making their case for mere-cognizance.

The classic Buddhist example of hungry ghosts seeing things differently from living humans does not carry much weight with people who don't believe in ghosts. A contemporary example might be more convincing. Philosopher Thomas Nagel presents an evocative description of a radically different way of experiencing the world from the way that it appears to us. He states:

I assume we all believe that bats have experience. After all, they are mammals, and there is no more doubt that they have experience than that mice or pigeons or whales have experience. I have chosen bats instead of wasps or flounders because if one travels too far down the phylogenetic tree, people gradually shed their faith that there is experience there at all. Bats, although more closely related to us than those other species, nevertheless present a range of activity and a sensory apparatus so different from ours that the problem I want to pose is exceptionally vivid (though it certainly could be raised with other species). Even without the benefit of philosophical reflection, anyone who has spent some time in an enclosed space with an excited bat knows what it is to encounter a fundamentally *alien* form of life.

I have said that the essence of the belief that bats have experience is that there is something that it is like to be a bat. Now we know that most bats (the *microchiroptera*, to be precise) perceive the external world primarily by sonar, or echolocation, detecting the reflections from objects within range, of their own rapid, subtly modulated, high-frequency shrieks. Their brains are designed to correlate the outgoing impulses with the subsequent echoes, and the information thus acquired enables bats to make precise discriminations of distance, size, shape, motion, and texture comparable to those we make by vision. But bat sonar, though clearly a form of perception, is not similar in its operation to any sense that we possess, and there is no reason to suppose that it is subjectively like anything we can experience or imagine.[6]

The bats' experience of reality must be as valid for bats as our experience is for humans, but what could these realities have in common? The bat example demonstrates that human perceptions cannot be based on extramental objects that really are the way we experience them.

In the first line of verse four of *Twenty Verses*, Vasubandhu uses dreams again to demonstrate that mere-cognizance can perform functions. His example is that mere images of sexual experience in dreams can produce bodily orgasms. Another example, that was not available to Vasubandhu, also makes this point. Think about all the appearances that arise on the screens that surround you and the many ways that these mere-cognizances shape your world.

Vasubandhu delivers his coup de grâce in the following verses. These contain debates about whether hell realms are external objective realities or merely mental appearances that arise due to previous actions (karma). In verse six, Vasubandhu suggests that rather than being constructed of physical matter, the hells are constructed from mind-stuff. He writes:

If you believe that the karma of hell-beings
Could produce physical matter and transform [it into hell
    realms],
Why do you not believe
That it is their consciousness that is being transformed?[7]

Vasubandhu's auto-commentary is even clearer. It asks, Why does the opponent fabricate concepts about physical matter as the basis for the arising of hell realms? The next verse points out that karmic results—the traces of our good and bad actions—are stored in the mind. It asks, Why would anyone expect these traces to mature someplace other than the mind?

The Name of This Tradition

We humans enjoy a good competition, and Buddhist panditas seem to be no exception. Despite their many common views and practices, the followers of Nagarjuna and those of Asanga and Vasubandhu evolved into players and cheerleaders for rival teams. In India and East Asia, the followers of Asanga and Vasubandhu were the New York Yankees, dominating their Mahayana rivals. It was only when Chandrakirti's Middle Way Mets arrived in Tibet that the Madhyamikas finally won their first World Series.[8]

Asanga and Vasubandhu did not set out to establish a distinct Mahayana school. The polemical relationship between their followers and the followers of the Middle Way didn't take shape until long after their time. It may well have come about because of the development of Buddhist scholarly institutions. In his introduction to his *Seven Works on Vasubandhu*, Stefan Anacker writes,

> It is true that present-day Tibetan classifications of Buddhist philosophy regard Nagarjuna and Vasubandhu as disagreeing. But these are really the disagreements of sixth-century followers of Nagarjuna and Vasubandhu. They belong to a

time when Buddhism had become an academic subject at places such as the University of Nalanda. They may have disagreed because they were academics fighting for posts and recognition.[9]

These conflicts overshadow the continuity between the two traditions and obscure the complementary nature of their insights. One relic of this rivalry is the different names we have for the Asanga-Vasubandhu tradition. The straightforward name for their school is Yogachara, or the "practice of yoga." This was originally a general term in India, without any doctrinal implications. It points to the system's origin in deep investigations of meditation experience, and it contrasts with the Madhyamaka school's greater reliance on logical reasoning.

More contentious names for the Asanga-Vasubandhu school are Chittamatra, or mind only,[10] and Vijnanavada, or proponents of consciousness. Both of these names suggest that the tradition is based on the belief that consciousness is ultimately real—a position that Asanga and Vasubandhu denied.

In *A Compendium of the Mahayana*, one of Asanga's major Yogachara treatises, he explains that mere-cognizance is only a provisional stage that bodhisattvas must progress through, declaring that they ultimately attain realization by "putting an end to the notion of mere cognizance too."[11] This is the same point Nagarjuna makes when he says that bodhisattvas need to abandon any concept of emptiness to realize complete freedom from fabrications.

Several verses in Vasubandhu's *Thirty Verses*[12] make the same point:

As long as the mind does not rest in mere-cognizance,
Tendencies of grasping to self and other will not cease.

Thinking that what is before you, "is just mere-cognizance,"
You do not abide in *suchness*.

When consciousness does not apprehend any object,
Because there is nothing to grasp, it rests in
   mere-cognizance.[13]

20

New Insights into Consciousness

With its unimpeded display seeming to appear
as [discrete] objects and perceiving subjects, this
naturally pure, unborn mind is ignorant of itself, of
its own essence. Just as water is [stirred] by waves,
[the alaya] is stirred by the motions of the seventh
mentation, which causes mind to form objects. On
the basis of that, [mind] becomes afflicted with [the
dualistic notions of] percepts and perceivers, and,
being deluded by that condition [that is, by afflictive
mentation], the imagination of what is unreal experiences the appearances of samsara.

Of what is [mind] ignorant? It is ignorant of mind-
itself, the heart of the buddhas, the display of the three
kayas. Why is it ignorant? Mind-itself is itself ignorant
because its unceasing expressive power appears to be
objects and perceiving subjects. It is ignorant because,
even though its essence does not exist as anything,
it conceives of its unified qualities—its unborn basic

nature and its unceasing brilliance—as self and other, respectively.

—The Third Karmapa and Jamgön Kongtrul[1]

EASTERN AND WESTERN thinkers have struggled to understand how the past, present, and future are connected. Clearly, there seems to be some relationship between what happened in the past and what is happening in the present, between what happens now and what will happen in the future. However, it isn't obvious how this could work.

The Buddha taught that what appears in the present depends on what appeared previously. This is what he called *pratitya-samutpada*, or dependent arising: all phenomena arise in dependence upon other phenomena. Many sutras recount the Buddha saying, "If this exists, that exists; if this ceases to exist, that also ceases to exist." He didn't explain how dependent arising works. As we have seen, the Buddha was pragmatic. His goal was to guide beings to freedom, not engage in philosophical speculation.

After the Buddha's time, a major school arose called Sarvastivada. The name of this school means "the theory that everything exists." (The Vaibhashikas, one of the abhidharma schools mentioned previously, were Sarvastivadins.) They argued that past dharmas were able to affect present dharmas because dharmas continue to exist in all three times. To explain how dharmas remain the same throughout the three times, and yet undergo change as they move from the future to the present and then into the past, Sarvastivadins held that dharmas have a constant essence that persists throughout the three times, but they only become "active" in the present.

Sautrantikas (the other abhidharma school mentioned previously) argued against this curious Sarvastivadin doctrine. They held that all dharmas are radically impermanent, disintegrating immediately upon arising. They argued that past dharmas could affect the present because disintegrating dharmas plant seeds in the stream of momentary consciousnesses and these seeds come to fruition when the appropriate conditions are present. These seeds are not entities but latent tendencies. Sometimes they spoke metaphorically of these tendencies "perfuming" the conscious continuum.

The Madhyamikas did not accept the ultimate existence of a stream of consciousness. In describing relative reality, some followed the explanations of the Sautrantika school, some followed the Yogachara school, and some merely followed worldly conventions. Generally, Madhyamikas are more concerned with presenting the ultimate emptiness of all phenomena than examining how dependent arising might work.

Memory

How do you think the past influences the present? Our memories seem to point to concrete past realities. But where are these realities located? When you think of your early childhood, it probably feels like something that really exists. I doubt that it feels imaginary—like unicorns or Peter Pan. But at the same time, you know that you can't have a conversation with your childhood mother as she was in her youth.

We moderns generally conceive of memory as a biological process, something that is outside of the mind, involving brains—physical matter. We should question that assumption. For instance, if you look in the refrigerator in the morning and realize that you are running out of milk or some other staple, this experience is purely a mental event. (Let's assume you don't write it on a shopping list or enter it in your phone.) As you return home that evening, you pass a grocery store, and the thought, "I need to buy milk," arises in your mind. This is another purely mental event. You might assume that the memory was stored in your brain all day long, but there is nothing in your direct experience that justifies this belief. The explanation is also a mental event. As far as your experience goes, everything took place in your consciousness. You don't have direct experience of the past, and you don't have direct experience of your brain.

The cognitive scientist Donald Hoffman provides a convincing argument against biological explanations of experience in *The Case Against Reality*.[2] He recounts an exchange with Nobel laureate Francis Crick, who contended that consciousness is merely a biological phenomenon. As Crick put it in his book *The Astonishing Hypothesis*, "'You, your joys and your sorrows, your memories and your ambitions, your sense of personal identity and free will, are in fact no more than the behavior of a vast assembly of nerve cells and their associated molecules.'"[3]

In an exchange of letters with Crick, Hoffman disputed this view:

> Crick claimed, and I agreed, that "seeing is an active, constructive process," that what we see "is a symbolic interpretation of the world," that "in fact we have no direct

knowledge of objects in the world," and that seeing is believing your best theory.

But then I set up my paradox. If we construct everything we see, and if we see neurons, then we construct neurons. But what we construct doesn't exist until we construct it. . . . So neurons don't exist until we construct them.

But this conclusion, I wrote in that March 22 letter, "contradicts, it would seem, the astonishing hypothesis, viz., that neurons exist prior to and are, somehow, causally responsible for, our perceptions."[4]

This contemporary analysis, based on the scientific study of perception, arrives at the same position that Mahayanists arrived at through reasoning and introspection.

The Framework of Eight Consciousnesses

Nagarjuna showed that everything that appears is empty; there is nothing that exists substantially, and mind is no exception. Mind is not substantial in any way, yet all of the diverse appearances of samsara and nirvana manifest from it. This raises a profound question: Since mind is not substantial, how could these appearances be produced?

Productive things always seem to be substantial. A computer screen is substantial. A television set is substantial. A phone is substantial. They each display lots of appearances. You might not have any idea how they work, but you know that they are machines, substantial machines. Anything you can think of that produces something is substantial. Otherwise you couldn't think of it.

There is no way to visualize how the empty mind produces appearances, yet that's exactly what it does. The mind is emptiness, yet thoughts, feelings, images, emotions, and sensory experiences all appear within it. Consciousness is a stream of emptiness. It is an ocean of emptiness, filled with all sorts of empty waves.

Vijnaptimatra—the principle of mere-cognizance—led Yogacharins to a deep examination of mind and its functions. They developed a framework of eight consciousnesses to explain how consciousness appears as the variety of outer and inner things. Earlier Buddhist schools described six consciousnesses: one consciousness connected with each of the five senses, plus a mental consciousness. In addition to these six active consciousnesses, Yogacharins described a seventh consciousness, *klishtamanas*, or afflictive mental activity, as well as an eighth consciousness, the *alayavijnana*, or the basis of all consciousness.

The alaya consciousness is presented as the storehouse of latent tendencies. Following the Sautrantikas, Yogacharins held that experience plants seeds in the mind. Contrary to the Sautrantikas, they argued that these seeds could not be stored in the active consciousnesses because these consciousnesses are momentary and unstable. That is why they posited the alaya as the repository of these imprints, as well as the locus for their subsequent manifestation. In Asanga's words,

> The alaya-consciousness's own characteristic is that it, based on the latent tendencies of all afflicted phenomena and by virtue of possessing [the capacity to] retain their seeds, is the very cause for their [future] arising.[5]

It is called the alaya, the ground of all, because all our experiences of homes, towns, relationships, conflicts, desires, hopes, fears, and even our self-images of body and mind emerge from it. They have no other basis. We have immediate experiences of sights, sounds, smells, tastes, tactile sensations, feelings, and thoughts, but these are mere appearances. They are not the substantial objects we conceive them to be. These sensory appearances are not the experiences of "things." They are merely dependently arisen appearances.

The seventh consciousness has two aspects. It causes appearances to arise from the alaya, and it is the basis of affliction. As such, it is referred to as *klishtamanas*, afflicted mental activity. We usually think that we continuously exist as perceiving subjects and perceived objects appear to us. Yogacharins realized that the feeling of subjectivity always arises simultaneously with the experience of objects. Perceiving subjects do not exist independently. The seventh consciousness moves the alaya, causing it to produce the appearances of subjects and objects, just as wind whips water into waves. Moving back and forth between outer and inner appearances, duality arises and solidifies. Both of these appearances are merely waves on the ocean of the alaya, stirred up by the movement of the seventh consciousness. The aspect that clings to the alaya as a self is the basis for affliction. Asanga describes the four afflictions of this consciousness as "views about a real personality, self-conceit, attachment to a self, and ignorance."[6]

The eight consciousnesses framework encompasses the totality of our experiences. Vasubandhu states this concisely in the *Thirty Verses*:

Whatever appears as "self" or "other" arises as a transformation of consciousness.
This transformation is of three kinds,

Maturation of latent tendencies, self-consciousness and cognition of sense objects.[7]

For practitioners, the eight-consciousness framework points out two essential aspects of our experience. One is that "the world" of experience is merely the maturation of seeds within the alaya. It is not the experience of a tangible, extramental world. The other is that the sensation of duality—an inner me-ness that seems to be experiencing outer objects and feels like such a solid, essential feature of reality—is just movements of mind, driven by the klesha consciousness.

Learning to distinguish these different aspects of experience is an essential step on the journey to freedom.

21

Three Natures

When we wrongly imagine there to be external objects we are led to think in terms of the duality of "grasped and grasper", of what is "out there" and what is "in here"—in short, of external world and self. Coming to see that there is no external world is a means, Vasubandhu thinks, of overcoming a very subtle way of believing in an "I" . . . once we see why physical objects can't exist we will lose all temptation to think there is a true "me" within. There are really just impressions, but we superimpose on these the false constructions of object and subject. Seeing this will free us from the false conception of an "I".

—*Mark Siderits*[1]

THESE ARE THE ELEMENTS of the Yogachara approach we have covered so far:

- The basis of their view is seeing that all experience is vijnaptimatra, mere cognition.

- Appearances are falsely conceived to be things outside of the mind.
- We mistake our fabricated world for an actual world. (There might be an extramental world, but it is nothing like the world of our projections, and even if there is such a thing, it is completely inaccessible to experience.)
- These fabrications conceal the basic, unfabricated ground that manifests as the diversity of experience.
- There are eight modes of consciousness, producing experiences of three types. First, there are the appearances that arise from the latent tendencies in the alaya, the all-ground. Second, there are afflictions of self-clinging, stirred up by the movements of afflicted mental activity. Finally, there are the sensory experiences of the active consciousnesses.

We have now arrived at the heart of the Yogachara approach— the imagination of the unreal. The displays of the eight consciousnesses are imagined to be a physical world out there and a mental world in here. All of these displays appear. All of them are falsely imagined to be what they are not.

Duality is intrinsic to the imagination of the unreal. Knower and known depend on each other. They are not separate entities but two aspects of each experience. The distinguished Buddhist scholar John Dunne describes the Yogachara presentation this way:

The sense of subjectivity in any moment of consciousness is simply a momentary "phenomenal form" or "image" (akara) that emerges simultaneously with the image or representation of the object. This "image" of subjectivity thus has no causal role or agency in that moment of visual perception; it instead reflects a basic structural feature—the subject-object relation—that characterizes any moment of consciousness bearing on an object.[2]

We never observe an object in an unperceived state, since the very process of observation means that consciousness is involved. We also never observe a consciousness that is not perceiving anything. Consciousness means to be aware of something.

Yogacharins use a scheme of three natures to explain delusion (the imagination of the unreal) and liberation (freedom from this delusion). The names of the three natures are the imaginary or fabricated nature (*parikalpita svabhava*), the dependent nature (*paratantra svabhava*), and the perfect nature (*parinishpanna svabhava*).

In his *Instruction on the Three Natures*,[3] Vasubandhu defines the dependent nature as what appears, the imaginary nature as the way it appears, and the perfect nature as the eternal absence of the way it appears in what appears.

The imaginary nature is the way dependent phenomena appear to deluded beings: as substantial outer and inner things, existing from their own sides. This duality only exists in our imagination.

The dependent nature consists of the mere appearances that arise to the eight consciousnesses and the eight consciousnesses themselves. These experiences are dependent because they depend on causes and conditions. They are not independently existing phenomena.

The perfect nature is that these phenomena never existed in the way they are imagined. There was never any duality existing in mere-cognizance. Recognizing this reveals the perfect nature. John Dunne writes:

> A metaphor used in Yogacara texts is helpful here. Suppose that a magician casts a spell on some stones such that his audience now sees them as elephants. The stones themselves represent the causal flow of mind. Those stones appear to the tricked audience as elephants, and this represents the constructed nature, namely, the fact that the mind itself (the stones) is appearing as something other than the mind (i.e., as elephants). The realization of the perfect nature is embodied by the magician who knows indubitably that he is actually seeing stones, which are empty of being elephants.[4]

The Elephant in the Room

The three natures presentation is not just another theoretical construct. It is a framework for investigating your experience that will guide you to profound insights. Jan Westerhoff explains this context:

> Yogacara arguments examine the various reasons we could give for why external objects exist, and the theories we develop about the existence of these objects, and show that the reasons do not justify our beliefs and that the theories are intrinsically problematic. This, however, does not lead to a kind of skeptical position where we have just refuted the claim that we have any knowledge of external objects, and must now suspend judgment about their real nature. Instead, the Yogacarin holds that once the erroneous

conceptions of reality have been cleared away, meditative practice will provide an avenue to gain a realization of their true nature. . . .

True philosophical insight, the Buddhist philosophers hold, does not come from studying a philosophical treatise, understanding its arguments, refuting objections, and assenting to its conclusions. What is at issue is the transformation of the way the world appears to us in our experience, not just of the way in which we think about the world that appears to us.[5]

Right now, it feels as if I am immersed in a world that extends beyond the sights, sounds, and tactile sensations that appear to my senses. There are no windows visible from where I am now working, but it seems like there's a house that I am sitting in, a garden outside, a street, a city, and a country "out there." There also seems to be a "me" who experiences all this "in here." What is all of this? It's the imaginary nature. It's mental images of things that I mistake to be something more than mere imagination. Recognizing that these experiences have always been free from duality is liberating, if only for a moment. This is the perfect nature. The power of latent tendencies quickly re-manifests, but the way forward is clear: by investigating the three natures again and again, delusion will diminish.

A few simple investigations might help you to explore this method. Begin by bringing to mind a meal you had yesterday.

What appears: a mental image of a meal
How it appears: as an event that you are recalling but that
  really existed at another time

The recollection of the meal is simply a dependently arisen mere-appearance, a movement of mind, like an image of something you experience in a dream. So is the self that seems to be recollecting that meal. Whatever theories you might have about how memory works, the recollection is not a substantial thing. It is a mental image. This is the dependent nature. The dualistic feeling that there is a real event that the memory refers to, and a substantial "me" who recalls that event, is the imaginary nature. The complete lack of this duality in the dependent nature is the perfect nature.

Next bring your awareness to any sensation of anxiety that you currently experience, or think of something stressful, and then rest right within the anxious feeling that arises.

What appears: an uncomfortable feeling
How it appears: as a feeling of distress that you are having
    caused by something really out there

When you experience anxiety, there are the mere feelings of anxiousness and a self who is suffering. These are the dependent nature. The imaginary nature is the sense that there is something out there that is causing distress and you in here who is experiencing it. The nonexistence of this duality in the dependent nature is the perfect nature.

Now examine the sound of a distant car or truck or something else that you hear in the environment.

What appears: a sound
How it appears: as a distant vehicle or something else that
    you are hearing

The dependent nature is the mere sound and the hearer of that sound before the sound is labeled "car" or "truck" or whatever. The imaginary nature is the traffic outside that you imagine is making that sound and the listener who is hearing it. The perfect nature is the absence of this duality in the dependent nature.

The Way Delusion Ceases

In the *Compendium of the Mahayana*, Asanga explains the way bodhisattvas develop penetrating insight into the perfect nature:

> They penetrate this just as in the case of a rope's appearing as a snake in a dark house. For example, [to see] a rope as a snake is mistaken because there is no [snake]. Those who realize this point end the mental state of [misperceiving] a snake where there is none and dwell in the mental state of [correctly perceiving] a rope. [However,] when taken in a subtle way, this is also mistaken because [a rope] consists of [nothing but] the characteristics of its color, smell, taste, and touch. [Thus,] based on the mental state of [perceiving] color and so on, the mental state of [perceiving] a rope is to be discarded too. Likewise, based on the mental state of [perceiving] the perfect nature, [any notion of] real referents with regard to the mental conceptions that appear as the six aspects of letters and referents is eliminated within those six aspects, just as the mental state of [misperceiving] a snake [is eliminated through correctly perceiving a rope]. Given that, the mental state of [perceiving] mere cognizance is also something that is to be dismantled.

Thus, through penetrating the characteristics of referents that are [nothing but] appearances of mental discourse, such bodhisattvas penetrate the imaginary nature. Through penetrating mere cognizance, they penetrate the dependent nature. "How do they penetrate the perfect nature?" They penetrate it through putting an end to the notion of mere cognizance too.[6]

22

We Are All Buddhas (with Stains)

Sentient beings are buddhas.
Nevertheless, they are obscured by adventitious stains.
When those are removed, they are buddhas.

—*Hevajra Tantra*[1]

TRADITIONAL DESCRIPTIONS of Asanga's meeting with Maitreya recount that when the great bodhisattva appeared, Asanga reproached him, saying, "You have no compassion! I have practiced so hard for twelve years and you never appeared. Why do you come only now?" Maitreya responded, "I have always been with you. Until now, your obscurations prevented you from seeing me."

These accounts go on to say that Asanga still had questions about the Mahayana teachings. Therefore, Maitreya had Asanga grasp his robes and ascended with him to his heavenly abode, where he taught him the contents of five texts that Asanga transcribed upon his return to this world. The Tibetan and Chinese versions of the *Five Treatises of Maitreya* only partially overlap, but both traditions regard these texts as authentic compositions of Maitreya himself.

Among the Maitreya treatises, the *Mahayanottaratantrashastra* (*Treatise on the Supreme Continuum of the Mahayana*), commonly referred to as the *Uttaratantra*, is one of the most profound and important texts of the Mahayana. The central theme of this text is *tathagatagarbha*, which is often translated into English as "buddha nature."[2]

Buddha Nature

That Maitreya is always present—but hidden—is a metaphor for buddha nature. Tathagatagarbha means that our essence is always the buddha qualities, but this essence is obscured by adventitious defilements—those that are not inherent or innate (the term *adventitious* comes from the Latin *adventicius*, meaning "coming from outside, external, foreign"). Another metaphor for buddha nature is the sun when it is concealed by clouds. The sun is always shining, but we cannot see it because the clouds block our view.

The tathagatagarbha teachings have profound implications. Because the qualities of buddhahood are essential to our being, four things follow:

- Those qualities are not something we create by practicing the path.
- Buddhahood is revealed by removing cognitive and emotional defilements, which are only incidental to our nature.

- Enlightenment is not produced by our practice.
- Because it is not a product, enlightenment is also not subject to decay.

The *Uttaratantra* uses various terms to refer to buddha nature. It is sometimes called the basic element, which points to buddha nature as the abiding nature of mind; sometimes it's called suchness with stains, to signify that it is the true nature of phenomena when they are covered by obscurations; sometimes it's called the disposition, to indicate buddha nature's role as the cause of awakening.

Two key verses in the *Uttaratantra* describe buddha nature:

There is nothing to be removed from this
And not the slightest to be added.
Actual reality is to be seen as it really is—
Whoever sees actual reality is liberated.

The basic element is empty of what is adventitious,
Which has the characteristic of being separable.
It is not empty of the unsurpassable attributes,
Which have the characteristic of being inseparable.[3]

This is the core message of the *Uttaratantra*—enlightenment is not some distant goal to be accomplished in the future. Buddhahood is not an extraordinary condition only obtained by the most worthy. Enlightenment and buddhahood have always existed, right *within* the delusions of living beings. Buddhahood is discovered by removing incidental stains. It cannot be created by any type of effort.

The *Uttaratantra* illustrates the way various stains conceal the buddha nature with a series of images from the sutras:

> A buddha in a decaying lotus, honey amid bees,
> Kernels in their husks, gold in filth,
> A treasure in the earth, a sprout and so on from a small
>   fruit,
> An image of the victor in a tattered garment,
>
> Royalty in the womb of a destitute woman,
> And a precious statue in clay—just as these exist,
> This basic element dwells in sentient beings
> Obscured by the adventitious stains of the afflictions.[4]

The first image, a buddha within a decaying lotus, symbolizes the way desire covers buddha nature (particularly when the desire's initial attraction fades). The second image, bees swarming around honey, symbolizes the way anger prevents us from tasting the sweet flavor of buddha nature. The third image, husks surrounding the germs of grains, symbolizes ignorance, which prevents us from extracting the nourishment from the kernels. The fourth image, gold buried in a place filled with excrement, symbolizes the active flaring up of the afflictions, which hides the gold-like buddha nature. The fifth image, a treasure beneath a poor person's house, symbolizes the richness that lies hidden within craving and dissatisfaction. The sixth image, the peel covering sprouts within tree fruit, symbolizes the potential for growing into a fully manifesting buddha, which lies concealed within the afflictions. The seventh image, the tattered garment covering the buddha image, symbolizes the way samsara can be revealed to be nirvana. The eighth image, a poor woman who will give birth to a great monarch, symbolizes the potential power that abides within our sense of powerlessness. The ninth image, a precious statue enclosed within a mold, symbolizes that the true nature of our minds is already perfected and ready to be revealed.

The Inexpressible

Contemplating these images should give you an impression of the way afflictions conceal buddha nature, but it's harder to get a feeling for what the afflictions conceal: the basic element or buddha nature itself. The stains are seemingly substantial, so material analogies make sense. Buddha nature is not substantial. Therefore, the images of statues and precious substances don't show us very much.

Buddha nature is the unconditioned ground of all. It is inexpressible spaciousness. It cannot be described by speech or captured by thought. It is empty of whatever we conceive it to be, yet it manifests as anything. It is the unfabricated basic ground for the arising of everything we could ever experience. It has qualities of expansiveness, of luminosity, of knowingness, of empty-cognizance.

The ultimate irony is that even the stains that obscure buddha nature are themselves nothing other than expressions of the unconditioned ground. It is because of this that liberation is possible. When the true nature of the stains is recognized, they *self-liberate*. That means they release themselves; they are not liberated by something external. One image for this is a snake uncoiling itself. Another image is waves that arise from and dissolve back into the ocean. When the stains self-liberate, buddha nature shines forth. It is as the great Indian siddha Saraha said: "By whatever it may be that fools are bound, through that, the wise become free swiftly."[5]

While stains conceal it, the basic element is always present as a potential. When the stains are removed, it is revealed to be the dharmakaya, or basic wisdom of a buddha.[6] Buddha nature does not change—before, during, or after. Its nature is always luminous emptiness.

The foundational teachings describe four mistaken conceptions that blind us to the true nature of phenomena:

Taking what is impermanent to be permanent;
What is suffering to be bliss;
What is impure to be pure;
What is not a self to be a self.

The ignorance at the root of these misconceptions is what causes us to wander in samsara. In order to help us overcome this ignorance, we are given four remedial conceptions. These concepts are antidotes for the four mistaken conceptions. They are the concepts that all phenomena are impermanent, suffering, egoless, and impure.

But even these four remedial conceptions do not describe the fruition of buddha nature. The dharmakaya of a buddha transcends permanence and impermanence, bliss and suffering, purity and impurity, self and selflessness. That is why the *Uttaratantra* describes the fruition in terms of four paramitas. Surprisingly, these are the paramitas of purity, self, bliss, and permanence.

The text explains:

Because the [dharmakaya] is naturally pure
And free from latent tendencies, it is pure.
It is the supreme self because the reference points
Of self and no-self are at peace.

It is bliss because the skandha of a mental nature
And its causes have come to an end.
It is permanent because the equality
Of samsara and nirvana is realized.[7]

23

Where Rubber and Road Meet

Usually, we tend to think of ourselves as really important. If we have any kind of suffering, we think that it is unbearable and that nobody else suffers as we do. We want to have happiness for ourselves and do not really consider that others feel the same. But the foundation for love, compassion, and bodhichitta is to think that others are equal to us and that we are able to exchange ourselves for them. Actually, to do this we have to rid ourselves of this notion that only we are important, that only our suffering is unbearable, and that our desire for joy is of paramount importance. How do we train our mind to do this? The first step is to realize: "If I feel that I am important and that my suffering is unbearable, then other beings must have the same attitude. When they suffer, they too must feel that this suffering is unbearable." This is the meaning of training the mind.

—*Khenchen Thrangu Rinpoche*[1]

SELF-DECEPTION IS one of the ego's most effective survival strategies. You can diligently study the dharma, contemplate its meaning, and meditate until smoke comes out of your ears, but if you don't put the dharma into practice in daily life, you'll be traveling the path to liberation with the emergency brake on. If you wish to overcome self-deception and progress rapidly along the path, it's essential to make the dharma a living experience.

It is said, "The best teacher is one who attacks your hidden faults; the best instruction is one aimed squarely at those hidden faults."[2] Here's an example from my own experience: I'm a critical person. It's easy for me to see the faults of others. But despite having sharp critical faculties, I often ignore the fact that fault-finding is itself a significant flaw, a stain that prevents me from seeing things as they really are. This is something I need to be on the lookout for.

You might have the great good fortune of meeting a human teacher who perfectly reflects your hidden faults, but such flawless mirrors are rare, and even if you connect with one, they might not be around when you need them. Fortunately, there are many teachings that can perform this function. There is a wonderful teaching called *The Seven Points of Training the Mind*, from the *lojong* (mind training) tradition, that the great Bengali master Atisha Dipankara brought to Tibet. It's shocking to me how many of my shortcomings have been exposed by this text, helping me to laugh at my ego's game and inspiring me to try to do better.

Bodhichitta

Atisha and his followers emphasized the cultivation of bodhichitta. *Bodhi* means "awakening" or "enlightenment" and *chitta* means "mind" or "heart." Together they mean something like "awakening mind" or "enlightened heart." Sometimes bodhichitta is described as the desire to attain complete, perfect buddhahood for the benefit of all sentient beings.

There are two aspects to bodhichitta: cultivating compassion and cultivating wisdom. These are known as relative and ultimate bodhichitta. *The Seven Points of Training the Mind* includes training in both, but it emphasizes the cultivation of compassion. This practice is extremely powerful because it goes against our self-centeredness and undermines habitual tendencies of ignoring the perspectives of others.

The text consists of fifty-nine slogans, or pith instructions, that are the basis for the training. Some of the slogans are instructions for formal meditation practice. Most are instructions for conduct in daily life. The way to work with this text is to first learn the slogans and then let them arise naturally in applicable situations. An easy way to learn the slogans is to regularly recite the root text. (The excellent translation by Trungpa Rinpoche and his Nalanda Translation Committee is included as appendix 2 in this volume. The Translation Committee also produces slogan cards and a poster, which can be helpful reminders to have around.) You could also study one of the many fine commentaries available in English that illuminate the meanings of the slogans.[3]

This chapter gives a summary of each of the seven points and some commentary on a selection of the slogans (based on the Nalanda Translation Committee's version of the text).

Point One—The Preliminaries, Which Are a Basis for Dharma Practice

First, train in the preliminaries.

The preliminaries are principally contemplating "four thoughts that turn the mind to the dharma." These are:

- Contemplating the good fortune of being born as a human, with good mental and physical faculties and a connection to the Mahayana dharma
- The inevitability of being separated from this life
- The inexorability of karma
- The inescapability of suffering in samsara

Our usual motivation is shortsighted. We concern ourselves with what we think will improve our lives in the coming hours, days, months, and years. We don't usually think about how transient and precious this life is and what we might face when it ends. No matter how much success we have in this life, and how much we manage to accumulate, none of it will provide lasting satisfaction, and we won't be able to take any of it with us. That's why practicing wholeheartedly is so essential.

Point Two—The Main Practice, Which Is Training in Bodhichitta

Regard all dharmas as dreams.
Examine the nature of unborn awareness.
Rest in the nature of alaya, the essence.

Training in absolute bodhichitta is the cultivation of wisdom. It is resting in basic mind, which is shamatha, and investigating the nature of whatever is experienced and the awareness that experiences it, which is vipashyana. The first slogans of this point are instructions in the essence of the practices of shamatha and vipashyana. The ultimate bodhichitta slogans precede the relative bodhichitta slogans because insight into emptiness and self-lessness is essential to give the practices of relative bodhichitta profundity and power.

Sending and taking should be practiced alternately. These two should ride the breath.

Training in relative bodhichitta is the cultivation of compassion. *The Seven Points of Training the Mind* offers a formal meditation practice to do this. It's known as *tonglen*. *Tong* in Tibetan means "sending," and *len* means "taking." Maybe not consciously, but on some level, we are always trying to take in what is good and give out what is bad. Tonglen practice reverses this samsaric logic. This is a meditation practice in which you breathe in other beings' difficulties and breathe your goodness out to them.

There are different instructions for doing tonglen. The way I was taught was that first you briefly recall ultimate bodhichitta—perhaps experiencing a glimpse of the primordial ground of luminous-emptiness. Next you visualize hot, thick, heavy air coming into you as you breathe in and cool, bright, light air leaving you as you breathe out. (Try not to speed up your breathing as you do this, but keep to a natural rhythm.)

After you've done this for a little while, think of something painful you've recently witnessed, and breathe that in. It could be a friend suffering some loss, a wounded animal, a person struggling with an illness or addiction—whatever image generates a feeling of empathy. Try to bring up something that provokes vivid experience, not just a general idea. As you breathe out, send that person or animal your well-being. After doing this for a while, think that there are other beings experiencing similar sufferings and include them in the exchange. Finally, breathe in all the suffering in this world, and breathe out general feelings of goodness and well-being. At the end of the session, let go of these visualizations, and rest in spaciousness for as long as you can. A session could last five minutes, half an hour, or whatever amount of time suits you.

Sometimes people worry that they might harm themselves by breathing in all this bad stuff. If you have these thoughts, remember that ultimately, this practice is working with your projections; they have no nature and cannot harm you. Conventionally, if you really could free other beings from suffering and at the same time free yourself from self-cherishing, why wouldn't you want to do that?

Point Three—Transformation of Bad Circumstances into the Path of Enlightenment

> When the world is filled with evil, transform all mishaps
> into the path of bodhi.
> Be grateful to everyone.

Here is a real challenge: Can you transform your attitude toward negative experiences? The setbacks and difficulties you encounter could become opportunities for practice, rather than obstacles to your journey. Usually, problems, difficult people, and painful situations seem like things we don't deserve. "Why is this happening to me?" The instruction here is to train in seeing that these experiences are not blocking your progress along the path. Quite the contrary—they are occasions for accelerating your progress through mind training. If you know how to use negative circumstances to practice relative bodhichitta, difficulties help you reduce ego-clinging and increase compassion. By resting right within the painful feelings, you can cut through karmic chain reactions. You might even recognize that the nature of these feelings is luminous-emptiness.

It is said that when Atisha was preparing to travel to Tibet, he heard that the Tibetans were kind and gentle people and worried that he wouldn't be able to practice relative bodhichitta. To make sure that he would have many opportunities to practice patience and compassion, he decided to take a short-tempered Bengali servant along as his attendant. When he finally arrived in Tibet and met the Tibetans, he realized he needn't have bothered!

Point Four—Showing the Utilization of Practice in One's Whole Life

Practice the five strengths, the condensed heart instructions.
The Mahayana instruction for ejection of consciousness at
    death is the five strengths: how you conduct yourself is
    important.

There are only two slogans in this section, and both involve the five strengths.

The first of the five strengths is *strong determination*. This is the commitment: "From this moment until enlightenment, at least from now until I die, and especially for the next year and the next month, and definitely from today until tomorrow,"[4] I will cultivate bodhichitta. The second strength is *familiarization*, gradually developing positive habits that counteract habits of mindlessness and self-centeredness. The third strength is called *seed of virtue*. This is keeping watch over your body, speech, and mind to make sure that your interactions with others are positive. The fourth strength is *reproach*. You reproach ego by thinking, "Previously, for time without beginning, you have made me wander in samsara and experience different kinds of suffering. In addition, all the suffering and evil that occur in this life are brought on by you."[5] The fifth strength is *aspiration*. After any virtuous activity, you dedicate whatever merit has been produced to the benefit of all beings.

The instructions for facing death in this tradition are also to practice the five strengths; then, "without clinging mentally to anything, one should rest evenly in a state of knowing that birth and death, samsara and nirvana, and so on, are all projections of mind, and that mind itself does not exist as anything."[6] Practicing these instructions will bring both types of bodhichitta to mind as you are dying.

Point Five—Evaluation of Mind Training

All dharma agrees at one point.
Of the two witnesses, hold the principal one.

How can you tell if you are progressing along the path? The point of dharma is to remove the ignorance of the nature of phenomena that is the cause of the kleshas and karmic actions that keep you wandering endlessly in samsara. Relative bodhichitta overcomes klesha and karma. Absolute bodhichitta overcomes ignorance of the true nature. To whatever extent you have diminished klesha and karma, and whatever extent you have recognized the true nature of phenomena, that is the extent of your progress along the path. In brief, we could simply say that the measure of your progress is how heavily you still cling to ego.

To clearly evaluate your progress, you need to root out any self-deception you have about being a good "dharma performer." You might get lots of positive feedback about being a good Buddhist, a good meditator, or a good teacher, but other peoples' feedback is only based on externals. Only you—the "principal witness"—can tell how much your ego has been tamed.

Point Six—Disciplines of Mind Training

> Change your attitude, but remain natural.
> Don't talk about injured limbs.
> Don't ponder others.
> Don't try to be the fastest.

The disciplines of relative bodhichitta are mainly concerned with tendencies to build ourselves up in relationship to other people. Instead of always putting yourself first, consider the needs of others. Abandon criticism of others. Don't try to get the better of them. And don't make a big deal of your virtue.

Point Seven—Guidelines of Mind Training

> All activities should be done with one intention.

This point conveys the overall spirit of lojong. That intention is kindness. Be kind to others. Be kind to yourself. You should give your ego a hard time, but still be kind to yourself!

24

Compassion in an Illusory World

I was flying recently from Los Angeles to Temuco, the largest city in the Araucanía region of Chile, when I got to thinking—as one inevitably does during globe-spanning flights—about the fallacy of maps.

In a way that is relatively novel in human history, people today are constantly bombarded with abstract representations of geography. Consider the red and blue of the polarized American electorate, the first-person view of a GPS navigator, and the blistering crimsons and oranges of global coronavirus hot spots.[1]

One understands, intellectually, that maps are mere representations, and that they may conceal as much as they illuminate. In "real life," states are neither red nor blue nor in any other way homogeneous; borders, in most places, do not exist other than in our minds, as the virus has made so tragically obvious. Yet when one experiences the world primarily through the mediated interfaces of our pocketable screens, such distinctions

tend to fall away. We live inside this digital world; it's
as real as anything else.

Believe it or not, these insights occurred to me
while playing a video game. . . . . I was not actually
flying from L.A. to Chile.

—*Farhad Manjoo*[2]

IF YOU STUDY the profound teachings, if you reflect on what
they mean, and if you meditate within this understanding,
you will catch glimpses of the illusoriness of this world. Seeing
the dreamlike nature of your projections, you will realize that
your version of the world is fabricated. You might be able to rest
within the spaciousness of this experience for some time. However, until you exhaust the latent tendencies of ignorance, you
will inevitably start reifying experience again and fall back into a
solid, habitual world.

That's okay. This alternation is an essential aspect of the journey. Insights from profound experiences will still be carried into
the rest of your life.

To work with the alternation, try to adapt your practice to your
actual level of insight. There's no point pretending that everything
is luminous-emptiness when you experience solidity and fixation.
Likewise, when you experience open spaciousness, you don't need
to cling to conventional practices. It's particularly important to
adapt compassion practice to your current level of insight.

Conventional compassion is a response to suffering that helps
us overcome indifference and enmity. At this level of practice, the

object of compassion, the compassionate person, and the suffering are all taken to be truly real. You cultivate this type of compassion by seeing how your own suffering and the suffering of others are essentially the same. This is called equalizing yourself and others.

When you see that the object of your compassion, the suffering, and you yourself are all illusory, you don't mistake *illusory* for *nonexistent*. You still practice compassion, but at this level, it is compassion for the mere appearance of suffering beings. You understand that until illusory beings recognize their own nature, their suffering will seem to them to be completely real. You attempt to remove the causes of their suffering, and ultimately to help them dispel the illusions.

The most profound level of compassion is nonreferential compassion in which there is no one cultivating anything, but there is spontaneous, effortless radiation of warmth and benefit for others. This is compassion that is inseparable from emptiness. It is the compassion of beings who have stabilized their realization.

Understanding these different ways of practicing will help you engage compassionately with the illusory world.

Living in the Illusion

In the *Fundamental Wisdom of the Middle Way*, Nagarjuna clearly emphasizes emptiness. But his teachings reveal more than just that. They also point out the inseparability of emptiness and dependent arising. This has deep practical significance: the more you understand emptiness, the more you will understand dependent arising. The more you understand dependent arising, the more you will know how to bring together causes and conditions that benefit beings without solidifying projections about what you are doing.[3]

There are so many beings who need our help. Trungpa Rinpoche put it vividly:

> This world needs tremendous help. Everybody's in trouble. Sometimes they pretend not to be, but still, there's a lot of pain and hardship. Everybody, every minute, is tortured, suffering a lot. We shouldn't just ignore them and save ourselves alone. That would be a tremendous crime.[4]

This applies to all the beings you encounter in your daily life: your family and friends; your dogs, cats, and hamsters; customer service people, salespeople, and tax collectors; pigeons, squirrels, and mosquitoes; homeless people and panhandlers.

Having mentioned homeless people and panhandlers, I feel compelled to mention Pope Francis's deep insights into how to really extend yourself to beings who are suffering:

> Speaking to the magazine *Scarp de' Tenis*, which means tennis shoes, a monthly for and about the homeless and marginalized, the Pope said that giving something to someone in need is "always right." . . .
>
> But what if someone uses the money for, say, a glass of wine? (A perfectly Milanese question.) His answer: If "a glass of wine is the only happiness he has in life, that's O.K. Instead, ask yourself, what do you do on the sly? What 'happiness' do you seek in secret?" Another way to look at it, he said, is to recognize how you are the "luckier" one,

with a home, a spouse and children, and then ask why your responsibility to help should be pushed onto someone else.

Then he posed a greater challenge. He said the way of giving is as important as the gift. You should not simply drop a bill into a cup and walk away. You must stop, look the person in the eyes, and touch his or her hands.

The reason is to preserve dignity, to see another person not as a pathology or a social condition, but as a human, with a life whose value is equal to your own.[5]

Beyond Imagination

Recognizing the illusoriness of our projected world should not blind us to the suffering that exists beyond our immediate experience. We can learn about the broader world through following the news, studying history, and listening to other people's stories. You might think that concentrating on your Buddhist practice is more important than engaging in such worldly activities, but taking in the suffering of the world will deepen your practice and your humanity and provide opportunities for developing deep compassion.

In broad strokes, there are three great domains of suffering in this world that we must face. Most obvious is warfare and the harm it causes to combatants, civilians, and the environment. More festering—but also deeply toxic—is the oppression, discrimination, and inequality that we humans foist on one another. Least visible, but perhaps ultimately most menacing, is the degradation of our environment, the decimation of entire species of plants and animals, and the decline in the livability of this planet caused by human activity.

Arne Naess, the Norwegian philosopher and a founder of the Deep Ecology movement, described these issues in an essay entitled "The Three Great Movements":

At the end of the twentieth century, we saw a convergence of three areas of self-destructiveness: the self-destructiveness of war, the self-destructiveness of exploitation and suppression among humans, and the self-destructiveness of suppression of nonhuman beings and of the degradation of life conditions in general. The movement to eradicate wars has a long history as a global movement. The movement against abject poverty and cruel exploitation and domination is younger. The third movement is quite young. These are the great movements that require intense participation on the grassroots level far into this new century.[6]

All these problems are driven by materialism. They are all *spiritual* problems at heart. Again, Trungpa Rinpoche's words point to the depth of these challenges:

When human beings lose their connection to nature, to heaven and earth, then they do not know how to nurture their environment or how to rule their world—which is saying the same thing. Human beings destroy their ecology at the same time that they destroy one another. From that perspective, healing our society goes hand in hand with healing our personal, elemental connection with the phenomenal world.[7]

25

The End

Joyful to have such a human birth,
Difficult to find, free and well-favored.

But death is real, comes without warning.
This body will be a corpse.

Unalterable are the laws of karma;
Cause and effect cannot be escaped.

Samsara is an ocean of suffering,
Unendurable, unbearably intense.

— "The Four Reminders"[1]

THE *Mahabharata*, the great ancient Indian epic, includes this interesting dialogue between Yama, the Lord of Death, and a prince named Yudhishthira. The prince asks Yama, "What is the most wondrous thing in this world?"

Yama replies, "Countless living beings meet death every day, yet those who remain behind believe themselves to be immortal and do not prepare for death. What can be more wondrous than this?"[2]

As a society, we put tremendous efforts into denying death, but death is clearly unavoidable. Whether you prepare for it or not, there will come a time when this life's appearances will disappear. Therefore, it would be better to be prepared.

It's not easy to contemplate your own mortality. When I was young, just hearing someone mention death put me in a tailspin. You too might have lots of energy invested in ignoring death. If you find you have a great deal of resistance to contemplating this, be gentle. Don't struggle with yourself, but come back to this reflection again and again until you develop some equanimity. As your emotional knots begin to untie, the release of bound-up energy might be painful. Don't be alarmed. This will pass, and the energy that was bound up in avoiding death will become available for living.

You might have concepts about what's going to happen when you die that come from science, from theology, or from culture more broadly. Holding fixed ideas (especially if they are soothing) will not be very helpful. To prepare properly for your death, examine whatever stories you tell yourself, and challenge your assumptions.

As you investigate, note that there are two different perspectives you can take toward the process. You can contemplate it from the outside, taking a third-person perspective. Or you can contemplate the process experientially from the first-person perspective. When preparing for your own death, the experiential perspective is the one that is vitally important.

Materialism and Death

Materialists look at death as a purely physical process—from the outside. Since they assert that everything real must be physical, they assume that the mind is extinguished when the body dies, and at that point, all experience comes to an end—like switching off a light. But since science cannot detect the presence of mind in living beings, how can it prove that mind is absent after death? From the third-person perspective, what evidence could there possibly be that mind ceases? It is certainly true that the *contents* of experience depend upon what appears to us as brains and sense organs. But that doesn't prove that mind itself is produced by something physical. As we have seen, all of our knowledge of the physical world, including brains and sense organs, is within mind.

I have already argued at length that the materialist position is incoherent. The assumption that experience ends at death, with no evidence to back it up, is a further sign of this incoherence. If materialists would think scientifically about death and question their assumptions, they would be, at the very least, agnostic about what comes after.

Theism and Death

Theists believe in divine beings, or cosmic principles, that are the cause of all that exists, including an essence—a soul, a spirit, or an atman—that continues beyond this life. Some believe that, because of their actions in this life, their essence will go to a Good Place (or maybe a Bad Place) after they die. Some believe that they will reincarnate for further lifetimes until they achieve liberation. These ideas are generally based on ancient revelations, handed down in holy books rather than personal experience.

When we thoroughly investigate with prajna, we find that no phenomena exist independently, including divine beings and cosmic principles; all phenomena are empty of what we conceive them to be. When we thoroughly investigate the self, we find no lasting essence. The souls, spirits, and atman that might continue into the afterlife are merely mental fabrications.

Buddhism and Death

Buddhist views of death do not fall into the extremes of either nihilism (the belief that there is nothing that continues after death) or eternalism (the belief that we have some lasting essence that continues after death). To understand how this could work, it is helpful to return to the teachings on buddha nature.

From a Mahayana perspective, dying is the disintegration of the seeming solidity of this life into the unconditioned ground of all: the dharmakaya, inexpressible spaciousness. This ground is not a thing. It is not a substance. It is complete emptiness. Yet it holds the latent tendencies for the manifestation of everything. This basic ground is what is continuous from one life to the next. Recognizing this basic ground is buddhahood. If we are well prepared, death becomes an opportunity for recognition.

There are guidebooks for the journey beyond this life that can help you contemplate what it will be like. The most well-known one is *The Great Liberation Through Hearing in the Bardo*, part of a rich cycle of teachings attributed to the great Buddhist master Padmasambhava. The title of this text was originally translated (and often still referred to) as *The Tibetan Book of the Dead*.

Dzogchen Ponlop Rinpoche explains the term *bardo* in his excellent contemporary guidebook, *Mind Beyond Death*:

> Whenever we embark on a long journey, there is a sense of death and rebirth. The experiences we go through have a transitional quality. The moment we step outside our house and close the door, we begin to leave our life behind. We say goodbye to family and friends and to the familiar rooms and routines that we inhabit. . . . Until we reach our destination, we are in transit—in between two points. One world has dissolved, like last night's dream, and the next has not yet arisen. . . .
>
> Leaving this life is similar in many ways to going on a long trip. In this case, the trip we are making is a journey of mind. We are leaving behind this body, our loved ones, our possessions, and all our experiences of this life, and moving on to the next. We are in transit, in between two points. We have left home but have not yet reached our next destination. We are neither in the past nor in the future. We are sandwiched between yesterday and tomorrow. Where we are now is the present, which is the only place we can be.
>
> This experience of the present moment is known as bardo in Tibetan Buddhism. Bardo in a literal sense means "interval"; it can also be translated as an "intermediate" or "in-between" state.[3]

Glimpses of the Journey

The journey beyond this life begins when we meet with conditions that will cause our death. This could be an illness, an accident, the failure of a vital organ, or the accumulated degenerations of old age. This stage of our journey is known as *the painful bardo of dying*. The texts describe this bardo as successive disintegrations of the elements that constitute the body.

At first there is a feeling of heaviness, as our strength, balance, and agility dissolve. It might become difficult to hold our heads up, or lift objects with our hands, or stand securely on our feet. At the same time, our perceptions start to dim and appearances become unclear.

Next, we might feel our mouth, nose, and tongue drying out, leaving us very thirsty. Mentally, we become agitated and confused, with vivid eruptions of emotionality.

After this, the heat of the body begins to dissipate. Our breath feels cold. Our extremities feel cold. The coldness spreads into our torso and into our hearts. This is accompanied by fluctuations of our mental clarity as we start to lose touch with our environment.

Next, breathing becomes difficult, and our thoughts become more vivid and disorienting. Eventually, breathing stops. From the perspective of others, death occurs at this point.

After this, all gross and subtle thoughts, together with dualistic mind itself, dissolve into the ground luminosity. This marks the end of the painful bardo of dying and the dawning of the *luminous bardo of dharmata*. If we recognize the ground luminosity at this point, we will be liberated. If not, we will faint and journey on.

Ponlop Rinpoche describes the possibilities in this way:

The arising of the ground luminosity signals the first stage of the bardo of dharmata. It is our first experience of the genuine luminosity of mind, its full state of wisdom. Viewed from the perspective of our practice and our spiritual journey, it is an extraordinary moment. It is the time when every aspect of the "all-basis consciousness," the *alayavijnana*, has dissolved into the fundamental state of wisdom, and we return to the original space of mind—its starting point. Since all aspects of our relative, conceptual mind have ceased, mind's absolute nature is revealed. Because that absolute nature is buddha nature, or *tathagatagarbha*, our experience in this moment is a vivid experience of enlightened mind. Even if we did not "get" the nature of mind in this lifetime, it manifests so powerfully now that we have a much greater opportunity to recognize it. . . .

If we can maintain our awareness now, then we can rest our mind in the ground luminosity, in the state of dharmata itself, which is said to be like a clear, cloudless sky—without sunlight, moonlight or starlight. It is a naked experience of awareness without any reference point, a pure experience of shunyata without a speck of obscuration.

Instead of going unconscious at this point, those who have a developed practice of meditation and have attained some realization of the nature of mind will recognize the ground luminosity as the fundamental nature of reality and the essence of their own minds. They will be able to rest in this luminosity. However, whether one is a practitioner or not, this experience of luminosity manifests unfailingly for all beings.[4]

If we fail to recognize our true nature and faint, the energy of the luminosity will again begin to stir. We will awaken to intense new experiences of "sights," "sounds," and "feelings." These appearances can take innumerable forms. The bardo teachings describe them as the successive manifestation of mandalas of peaceful and wrathful deities, but this iconography symbolizes qualities of the experiences, not actual forms of beings that will appear. Because the raw intensity of these experiences won't be buffered by having a body and a sensory environment, the intensity will be hallucinatory and overwhelming. If we have not trained in resting right within vivid feelings and emotions during this lifetime, it will be extremely difficult to recognize these experiences as the spontaneously arising luminosity of our own minds. If we can recognize the displays of luminosity at this point, we will be liberated. If not, we will again lose consciousness and journey on.

Arising from this swoon, we will compulsively seek shelter from the intensity. This marks the beginning of the *karmic bardo of becoming*, which will continue until we meet with the conditions that will lead to our next rebirth.

The Opportunity

Generally, death seems to be the ultimate threat, something we need to avoid at all costs, and yet death is patently and potently inevitable. The point of studying the bardo teachings is that the journey beyond this life can be taken as path. As Ponlop Rinpoche points out, for practitioners, death is an opportunity:

When we can be fully present with them, the experiences we meet throughout the bardos of death become simple and natural. We can actually afford to relax and let go of hope and fear. We can be inquisitive about our new experiences. We can also learn something about ourselves—that ultimately, who we are in the most genuine sense transcends our limited notion of self. At this transitional point, we have an opportunity to go beyond that perception and transform the appearance of death into an experience of awakening by recognizing the true nature of mind. . . .[5]

. . . Rather than feeling, "Oh no, I don't want to be here," we should be full of enthusiasm and curiosity. We should resolve to remain calm and to be courageous. It is like exploring any new place.[6]

Of course, changing your attitude toward death won't happen just by snapping your fingers. You need to reflect on this journey many times, until it really makes sense to you.

This notion of inquisitiveness and bravery applies not only to the journey from death to rebirth. It also applies to the journey of this life. As practitioners, we are often held back by longing for some future liberation. Hopes and fears about the future overshadow and obscure what we are experiencing right now. The fundamental message of the Mahayana is that this is a journey of discovery. You don't need to fabricate anything to reach liberation. The fruition is already within you, waiting to be discovered.

Epilogue

If I ever go looking for my heart's desire again, I won't
look any further than my own backyard. Because if
it isn't there, I never really lost it to begin with . . .
There's no place like home.

—Dorothy, in The Wizard of Oz

APPENDIX 1

Contemporary Thinking about Mind and Nature

There are good reasons why you might want to understand contemporary thinking about mind and nature. For one thing, reflecting on these various philosophical positions can help you develop new insights into the nature of reality. For another, understanding these views could facilitate meaningful conversations with scientists and other intellectuals. Finally, these approaches are provocative and fascinating—at least they are to me.

To begin, we need to know who the metaphysical dogs are in this race. They fall into four groups:

- Those who regard the physical as the only reality
- Those who regard the physical and mental as different but interacting realities
- Those who regard the physical and mental as two different aspects of a common underlying reality
- Those who regard the mental as the only reality

We've already examined materialism, the view that the physical is the only reality, in chapters 9–11. Now we'll look at the other positions. Try not to jump to conclusions about which approach is *right*. It's more useful to reflect on each position and look into your own experience to see what it would mean for a particular position to be true and what the implications of that truth might be. When you look into the arguments, look loosely. Many of the concepts are subtle. Use your antennae to get a feeling for the position. You don't need to absolutely nail everything down.

Four Alternative Mind-Body Relationships

	MENTAL	PHYSICAL
MATERIALISM/PHYSICALISM Physical realm is real; mental realm is an illusion or nonexistent.	○	■
DUALISM Physical realm and mental realm are both real substances that interact.	●	■
PANPSYCHISM/COSMOPSYCHISM The inner nature of the physical is mental.	●	
IDEALISM Mental realm is real; physical realm is an illusion or nonexistent.	●	□

MIND-BODY DUALISM

If I asked you whether your mind and your body were substantially different—or, more particularly, if your mind and your brain were different things—I'm pretty sure that, without too much reflection, you would say that they were: "Of course, my brain is physical, and my mind is not!"

There is a strong intuitive appeal to mind-body dualism. Most of us believe that we have both minds and bodies and that minds and bodies obviously interact. Our mental experiences are influenced by the physical world, and we often have physical reactions to mental experiences. Bodily feelings of hunger cause us to eat, and so does the idea "it's lunchtime." Thinking about painful experiences can make our stomachs churn, and thinking about people we love can cause us to relax.

A common objection to dualism is that it is impossible for physical bodies and immaterial minds to interact. You might challenge the plausibility of mind-body dualism by asking such questions as: How is mind-body interaction possible? Where does the interaction occur? What is the nature of the interface between mind and matter? How are volitions translated into states of affairs? Aren't minds and bodies insufficiently alike for the one to effect changes in the other?

One way of responding to this challenge is to note that the notion of interaction is not merely a matter of mechanical connection. For example, interactions in quantum physics, where presumably the rubber of mind would meet the road of matter, include, as science author Adam Becker puts it, such weird events as "atoms that are here and there at the same time, radiation that has both been emitted and remains latent in its source . . . [and] long-distance connections between objects."[1]

Also, as philosopher Scott Calef writes,

It is useful to be reminded, however, that to be bewildered by something is not in itself to present an argument against, or even evidence against, the possibility of that thing being a matter of fact. To ask "How is it possible that . . . ?" is merely to raise a topic for discussion. And if the dualist doesn't know or cannot say how minds and bodies interact, what follows about dualism? Nothing much. It only follows that dualists do not know everything about metaphysics. But so what? Psychologists, physicists, sociologists, and economists don't know everything about their respective disciplines. Why should the dualist be any different?[2]

CARTESIAN DUALISM

The type of dualism that most contemporary critiques target is based on conceptions that go back to René Descartes, who is widely considered to be the father of modern philosophy. In his most important work, *Meditations on First Philosophy* (what is now called metaphysics), Descartes concluded his investigations by reasoning that since mind is utterly indivisible and material things are divisible, mind and body must be entirely different substances. He inferred that these two substances must interact in the brain. This substance dualism is now referred to as Cartesian dualism.

It is hard to know what substance means when thinking about the mind. For Descartes, it is clear that this substance is the self, or the soul. For Buddhists and some Western thinkers, it seems clear that no such self or soul can be found. In chapter 6, we looked into this issue from a Buddhist perspective. David Hume, the great eighteenth-century Scottish philosopher, presented arguments against both substances and a self in *A Treatise of Human Nature*. His assessment of the intelligibility of the concept of self is similar to Buddhist arguments:

> For my part, when I enter most intimately into what I call myself, I always stumble on some particular perception or other, of heat or cold, light or shade, love or hatred, pain or pleasure. I never can catch myself at any time without a perception, and never can observe any thing but the perception.[3]

When materialists argue against dualism, it is usually substance dualism that they are contesting. The attack usually takes this form: "We now know all the basic particles and forces in the universe, and supernatural mental substances that dualists imagine do not exist." The weakness of this materialist argument is that it fails to acknowledge that all those particles and forces are known by the mind they are trying to refute.

Cartesian dualism is not the only form of mind-body dualism. Some philosophers object to the possibility of a duality of substances, but do not deny that mind and matter have different properties. These *property dualists* maintain that there is only one kind of substance but agree that there are fundamental differences in the properties of mind and matter.

All proponents of dualism face an explanatory gap that is just as wide as the explanatory gap faced by proponents of materialism, but they are at least saved the embarrassment of trying to explain away the experience of consciousness.

Materialists do hold one advantage in the debate with dualists: the prevailing scientific-materialist intellectual climate. In their introduction to an anthology of modern approaches to mind-body dualism, Andrea Lavazza and Howard Robinson write that there is:

> a contemporary intellectual culture that seems to regard dualism as suspicious at best if not entirely misguided. . . . But the attacks are often dismissive, and the arguments are met without difficulty. Indeed, the present situation indicates that mental-physical dualism has fallen into disfavour in the contemporary intellectual scene not because the arguments for it have been found to be faulty but because it is assumed not to fit, or fit sufficiently well, with the naturalist perspective that the advance of science had made seem so irresistible.[4]

WHAT IS THE NATURE OF MATTER?

Substance dualism highlights puzzling questions about the nature of mind. It also leads into equally puzzling questions about the nature of matter.

Our commonsense view of matter—that we are surrounded by a world of lasting, substantial objects that exist independently of our experience—is challenged both by Buddhism and by modern physics. To understand the challenge from the side of science, we need to look at a bit of history.

The scientific view of matter has evolved dramatically since the dawn of the Scientific Revolution. Descartes and his successors viewed the physical world as a machine. Physical objects interacted by direct contact or impact. Matter could be divided and quantified. Material things were characterized by their extension in length, breadth, and depth; by having various parts with sizes, shapes, positions, and motions; and by having various definite durations in time. The material world was the subject matter of pure mathematics.

Galileo elegantly described the need for mathematics in reading the book of nature:

> Philosophy [i.e., natural philosophy] is written in this grand book — I mean the Universe — which stands continually open to our gaze, but it cannot be understood unless one first learns to comprehend the language and interpret the characters in which it is written. It is written in the language of mathematics, and its characters are triangles, circles, and other geometrical figures, without which it is humanly impossible to understand a single word of it; without these, one is wandering around in a dark labyrinth.[5]

Less than a century after Descartes and Galileo, the mechanical conception of the natural world was undermined by Isaac Newton's law of universal gravitation. His mathematical model of gravity showed that physical interaction took place at a distance, without contact. The law states that everything in the universe exerts forces on everything else. It quantifies the force of gravity and tells us what gravity *does*—but not what gravity *is*.

Early in the twentieth century, physicists' understanding of nature took a further turn toward abstraction. In 1905, Albert Einstein published a landmark paper on special relativity that demonstrated that time and length are relative to the frame of reference of the observer. While this would only be apparent at extreme velocities—velocities approaching the speed of light—it eroded the Newtonian notions of absolute time and space. This was the beginning of what is now considered to be modern physics. To accommodate this new understanding, physicists developed four-dimensional geometric representations of *spacetime* that mathematically combine our ordinary conception of three-dimensional space with the dimension of time. Spacetime subsequently became the foundation for Einstein's general theory of relativity.

The development of quantum physics further undermined commonsense conceptions of the fundamental nature of matter. Adam Becker writes:

Quantum physics—the physics of atoms and other ultratiny objects, like molecules and subatomic particles—is the most successful theory in all of science. It predicts a stunning variety of phenomena to an extraordinary degree of accuracy, and its impact goes well beyond the world of the very small and into our everyday lives. The discovery of quantum physics in the early twentieth century led directly to the silicon transistors buried in your phone and the LEDs in its screen, the nuclear hearts of the most distant space probes and the lasers in the supermarket checkout scanner. Quantum physics explains why the Sun shines and how your eyes can see. It explains the entire discipline of chemistry, periodic table and all. It even explains how things stay solid, like the chair you're sitting in or your own bones and skin. All of this comes down to very tiny objects behaving in very odd ways.[6]

Like Galileo and Newton's explanations before them, quantum explanations take the form of sophisticated mathematical equations. Beyond the math, there are no commonly accepted explanations of the nature of all these particles and forces. Today, more than a century after the dawn of quantum physics, if a physicist asks, "What is this stuff that all our equations describe?" the standard answer is, "Shut up and calculate!"

The philosopher Bertrand Russell described the enigma of the quantum view of matter elegantly: "It has begun to seem that matter, like the Cheshire Cat, is becoming gradually diaphanous until nothing of it is left but the grin, caused, presumably, by amusement at those who still think it is there."[7]

PANPSYCHISM

Modern physics dramatically changed science's view of matter, which also offered new possibilities for understanding mind's relationship to nature. Some of these approaches fall within the view called *panpsychism*. The literal meaning of panpsychism is that everything has a mind, but the term is used more broadly to describe a range of views that consider mind to be fundamental and pervasive in the natural world. It isn't necessary to believe that stones and trees have experiences to be a panpsychist, but at least the fundamental constituents of the rocks and trees must have mental properties.

While this claim might seem extremely counterintuitive, it has a certain logical appeal when contrasted with other approaches we have considered. Unlike dualism's hard distinction between the mental and physical realms, panpsychism offers a unified view of nature. And unlike the eliminativist and reductionist views of materialism, panpsychism takes subjectivity seriously.

Panpsychism is a general approach to understanding the natural world, rather than a specific theory. Within this general approach, there are diverse theories about what this fundamental union might be like.

NEUTRAL MONISM

Although there is a long history of panpsychism in both Eastern and Western philosophical thought, this view has undergone radical changes in the modern era. Around the turn of the twentieth century, as modern physics began to emerge, Bertrand Russell, William James, and Ernst Mach developed a view called *neutral monism*. The core of this view is that both physical and mental phenomena arise from a single reality (this is the monism aspect) that is neither physical nor mental (this is the neutral aspect).

Though each of these thinkers used different terms to describe this single reality, what they all described was subjective experience—"what is most indubitable in our knowledge of the world."[8] In contrast to the undeniable reality of direct experience, they maintained that the experiencer, and the things experienced, are abstractions.

Conventionally, we view experience as having three aspects: there is someone having the experience, something that is being experienced, and the experience itself. For example, when someone hears the sound of a passing car, we assume that there is something making the sound, someone hearing the sound, and the experience itself. But the neutral monists argue that when you investigate this experience, you only find the experience of sound; what James called "pure experience." The passing car only exists as an inference, a conceptual construct. Likewise, the self that is supposedly hearing the sound cannot be found outside of the hearing itself. Similarly, when someone sees a bright red object, there's a vivid experience, but no object apart from the perception and no one experiencing the object that is separate from the experience itself.

The ego, or the self, in Russell's words, "embodies a belief in substance which we must shut out of our thoughts."[9] Our knowledge of the physical world is also purely inferential and abstract. "We know certain logical characteristics of its structure, but nothing of its intrinsic character."[10] (This is similar to the Buddhist approach of distinguishing perception from conception that we looked at in chapter 5, and the investigations of selflessness in chapter 6.)

The neutral monists reasoned that experience can be understood from either "mental" or "physical" perspectives, depending on the way it is investigated. You can look at the physical characteristics of a sound—its source, its frequency, and so on. You can also look at the psychological aspects of the sound—its pleasantness, its ability to provoke memories, and so on. Russell writes:

A piece of matter is a group of events [experiences] connected by causal laws, namely, the causal laws of physics. A mind is a group of events connected by causal laws, namely, the causal laws of psychology. An event is not rendered either mental or material by any intrinsic quality, but only by its causal relations. It is perfectly possible for an event to have both the causal relations characteristic of physics and those characteristic of psychology. In that case, the event is both mental and material at once. There is no more difficulty about this than there is about a man being at once a baker and a father. Since we know nothing about the intrinsic quality of physical events except when these are mental events that we directly experience, we cannot say either that the physical world outside our heads is different from the mental world or that it is not. The supposed problem of the relations of mind and matter arises only through mistakenly treating both as "things" and not as groups of events.[11]

In this way, neutral monists attempt to dissolve the mind-body problem by showing that things we call mind and things we call body are both conceptual constructs, and not concrete features of the natural world. "An isolated ego exists no more than an isolated object: both are provisional fictions of the same kind."[12]

Neutral monism was central to philosophical discussions of the integration of mind and matter until the 1930s, when materialism began to dominate the philosophy of mind, and behaviorism began to dominate the study of psychology. Toward the end of the twentieth century, interest in panpsychism began to revive, as the continuing failure of materialists to come up with satisfying accounts of consciousness encouraged philosophers to look for alternative approaches.

PHYSICALISM RECONSIDERED

Although neutral monism is a compelling and elegant way of viewing the integration of mind and matter in nature, more recent panpsychists have searched for tighter connections between the material and the mental. These panpsychist theories attempt to ground this union in quantum physics, information theory, neuroscience, and other theoretical models.

One of the more interesting panpsychist approaches is Galen Strawson's *real physicalism*. Strawson is an English philosopher who is both eloquent and witty. He has written acerbic critiques of the materialists. Like the neutral monists, his metaphysics begins with experience:

> What people almost always mean, when they say that consciousness is a mystery, is that it's mysterious how consciousness can be simply a matter of physical goings-on in the brain. But here they make a very large mistake, a "Very Large Mistake", in Winnie-The-Pooh's terminology—the mistake of thinking we know enough about what physical stuff is to have good reason to think that physical goings-on in the brain can't be conscious goings-on. A good number of philosophers have based their careers on this mistake, and they can't now turn back, but the truth is that the fundamental stuff-nature of physical being is unknowable—except insofar as it is consciousness. If you doubt this, ask some thoughtful physicists.[13]

Strawson, like other panpsychists, takes consciousness to be a fundamental feature of reality. He argues that any understanding of the natural world must start from accepting the reality of experience:

> Full recognition of the reality of experience, then, is the obligatory starting point for any remotely realistic version of physicalism. This is because it is the obligatory starting point for any remotely realistic (indeed any non-self-defeating) theory of what there is. It is the obligatory starting point for any theory that can legitimately claim to be "naturalistic" because experience is itself the fundamental given natural fact; it is a very old point that there is nothing more certain than the existence of experience.[14]

Strawson takes consciousness seriously, and he also takes physics seriously. His physicalism is "real physicalism" because it encompasses both mind and matter, unlike the "faux-physicalism" of the materialists. Like the neutral monists, he is clear about what physics can tell us about physical reality, as well as what it cannot. He writes:

> We don't see that the hard problem is not what consciousness is, it's what matter is—what the physical is. We may think that physics is sorting this out, and it's true that physics is magnificent. It tells us a great many facts about the mathematically describable structure of physical reality, facts that it expresses with numbers and equations (e = mc², the inverse-square law of gravitational attraction, the periodic table and so on) and that we can use to build amazing devices. True, but it doesn't tell us anything at all about the intrinsic nature of the stuff that fleshes out this structure. Physics is silent—perfectly and forever silent—on this question.[15]

The central premise of real physicalism is that the intrinsic nature of at least some of physical reality must be mental or experiential—since we know this from our own case. We also find nothing in physics that gives us reasons to believe that there is any *non*-experiential physical reality. Real physicalism is the "have your cake and eat it" option: you get all the physical reality of materialism, and all the mental reality of idealism, with none of the metaphysical calories of either.

An important argument for real physicalism (and for panpsychism in general) is that it avoids one of the more incoherent elements of materialism. Unless materialists deny consciousness completely, they must believe that somewhere in the course of evolution, mind arose from mindless matter. This is not only a historical issue. Such radical emergence must happen every day. If a human egg does not have mind and a newborn infant does, when and how does mind emerge? No one seems to offer a convincing explanation of how this might work.

While the unified picture of the natural world presented by panpsychism has a certain appeal, these theories also raise serious objections.

For one thing, it is highly counterintuitive to think that the fundamental constituents of reality are mental. Is it really the case that quarks and photons have experience? What on earth could this be like? On the other hand, it seems no harder to conceive of experiential photons than it is to conceive of the fundamental components of reality as quantum fields that behave like both particles and waves, that have uncertain locations, and that can entangle each other over vast distances—and these are all accepted elements of contemporary physics.

A greater challenge to panpsychism is the combination problem: how can discrete micro-experiential subjects combine to produce the unified field of subjectivity that we experience? Critics contend that this is a knockout blow against panpsychism. They argue that the combination problem produces an explanatory gap that is just as deep as the materialists' explanatory gap of subjectivity arising from nonexperiential matter.

Strawson responds that solving the combination problem might seem inconceivable to us now, but it must not be fundamentally different from the problem of understanding the way elementary particles combine to make complex forms, such as ourselves and the world around us. He says:

> Once upon a time there was relatively unorganized matter, with both experiential and non-experiential fundamental features. It organized into increasingly complex forms, both experiential and non-experiential, by many processes including evolution by natural selection. And just as there was spectacular enlargement and fine-tuning of non-experiential forms (the bodies of living things), so too there was spectacular enlargement and fine-tuning of experiential forms.[16]

As Strawson acknowledges, this is a framework for a response "at a very high level of generality." For panpsychism to gain traction, the combination problem must be addressed by coming up with an adequate account of how mental combination could occur. This is a challenge that is the focus of much of contemporary panpsychist research.

INTEGRATED INFORMATION THEORY

There's one more approach within the general region of panpsychism that should be mentioned. Over the past few years, Giulio Tononi's Integrated Information Theory (IIT) has attracted a lot of attention. No doubt this is because it is the rare neuroscientific theory that takes the reality of experience as its starting point. But it's also because of the support and collaboration of the influential neuroscientist Christof Koch. Interest in IIT hasn't been confined to science and philosophy circles. Popular articles have also appeared in the NY Times,[17] the New Yorker,[18] and Scientific American.[19]

IIT doesn't really attack the hard problem. Instead, it asks, "Given what we know to be the essential properties of consciousness, what features must physical systems supporting consciousness have?" The theory lays out a series of axioms about consciousness, and then postulates properties that the physical systems must have to support it. IIT claims that, at the fundamental level, consciousness is integrated information and that its quality and quantity can be understood from the informational relationships generated by a complex of physical elements. It proposes a measure of the quantity of consciousness that a physical system supports based on the degree to which the system integrates information. An example that Tononi and Koch use to support the theory is that brain research shows that the human cerebral cortex appears to be deeply connected with consciousness. The cerebral cortex is also structured to integrate a great deal of information. The cerebellum does not appear to contribute to consciousness, despite having many more neurons than the cerebral cortex, and these neurons are not interconnected in the same elaborate ways that the neurons in the cerebral cortex are.

IIT is usually included in lists of panpsychist theories because it treats consciousness as a fundamental property of reality. It suggests that consciousness is likely to be widespread among animals, and that it can be found in small amounts even in certain very simple systems. However, IIT does not fit most definitions of panpsychism because it implies that not everything is conscious.

While Tononi and Koch claim that IIT describes what consciousness is, it seems that something has been lost in translation. By declaring that consciousness *just is* integrated information, IIT looks a lot like other reductionist theories of consciousness.

IDEALISM

David Chalmers began his recent article "Idealism and the Mind-Body Problem" with this anecdote:

> When I was in graduate school, I recall hearing "One starts as a materialist, then one becomes a dualist, then a panpsychist, and one ends up as an idealist". I don't know where this comes from, but I think the idea was something like this. First, one is impressed by the successes of science, endorsing materialism about everything and so about the mind. Second, one is moved by the problem of consciousness to see a gap between physics and consciousness, thereby endorsing dualism, where both matter and consciousness are fundamental. Third, one is moved by the inscrutability of matter to realize that science reveals at most the structure of matter and not its underlying nature, and to speculate that this nature may involve consciousness, thereby endorsing panpsychism. Fourth, one comes to think that there is little reason to believe in anything beyond consciousness and that the physical world is wholly constituted by consciousness, thereby endorsing idealism.[20]

Now we've arrived at idealism. Perhaps you've gone through a similar progression of insights to get here.

Empiricism was an eighteenth- and nineteenth-century philosophical movement that maintained that sensory experience was the basis for all knowledge. In the Western tradition, the British Empiricists, notably George Berkeley and David Hume, were proponents of what we now call idealism.

George Berkeley, episcopal bishop of Cloyne, was an Irish philosopher and theologian. His most important work, *A Treatise Concerning the Principles of Human Knowledge*, argued against the existence of material substances. This thesis, which he called *immaterialism*, maintained that all objects of experience are merely ideas in the minds of perceivers. Berkeley wrote:

> I do not argue against the existence of any one thing that we can apprehend, either by sense or reflexion [reflection]. That the things I see with mine eyes and touch with my hands do exist, really exist, I make not the least question. The only thing whose existence we deny, is that which philosophers call matter or corporeal substance. And in doing of this, there is no damage done to the rest of mankind, who, I dare say, will never miss it.[21]

Berkeley begins the *Principles* with an extended critique of abstract ideas, claiming that they are the source of all philosophical confusion, contradictions, and errors. In broad strokes, his argument is that abstract entities are impossible, and therefore the mind can't form abstractions concerning these nonentities. For example, you can think of the abstraction "color," but there is nothing that this corresponds to—that is *just color*—without being a particular color, such as red, green, yellow, or blue. When you look at an actual apple, it appears to be certain shades of red. You can have an idea of the color red based on this experience. However, the abstract idea of color does not have any basis. There is nothing in your experience for the idea to indicate.

This leads to Berkeley's core argument: we only know that things exist if they can be perceived, which he expresses with the phrase *esse est percipi*—to be is to be perceived. His reasoning for this assertion begins by acknowledging that people normally believe that things really do exist, whether they are perceived or not. But then he asks, What are these existing things besides our sensory experiences of them? He states:

> It is indeed an opinion strangely prevailing amongst men, that houses, mountains, rivers, and in a word all sensible objects have an existence natural or real, distinct from their being perceived by the understanding. But with how great an assurance and acquiescence soever this principle may be entertained in the world; yet whoever shall find in his heart to call it in question, may, if I mistake not, perceive it to involve a manifest contradiction. For what are the forementioned objects but the things we perceive by sense, and what do we perceive besides our own ideas or sensations; and is it not plainly repugnant that any one of these or any combination of them should exist unperceived?[22]

Berkeley then addresses an objection that what we experience are representations; they are not the things themselves, but rather, they are *like* the things that really do exist independently of our minds. Positing such a resemblance, he argues, does not make sense. A representation and a thing represented cannot be alike. There can be no likeness between an idea and a nonexperienced, mind-independent object, since such an object is never experienced and the two things can never be compared. "An idea can only be like another idea; a colour or figure can be like nothing but another colour or figure"[23]

Next, he points to the materialists' explanatory gap: that the belief in a mind-independent world does not help to explain experience. He states:

> Though we give the materialists their external bodies, they by their own confession are never the nearer knowing how

our ideas are produced: since they own themselves unable to comprehend in what manner body can act upon spirit, or how it is possible it should imprint any idea in the mind. Hence it is evident the production of ideas or sensations in our minds, can be no reason why we should suppose matter or corporeal substances, since that is acknowledged to remain equally inexplicable with, or without this supposition.[24]

David Hume (whom we encountered briefly above) was strongly influenced by Berkeley. In *A Treatise of Human Nature*, he takes a similar tack, challenging the existence of mind-independent substances. Where Hume and Berkeley part ways is in their beliefs about the nature of perceivers. For Berkeley, the mind, or spirit, is a substantial thing that actually exists (as does God—the ultimately existing perceiver). For Hume, even the existence of a perceiver is suspect.

Instead of this unfindable, continuous thing called a self, Hume proposes a bundle theory of perception: we are bundles of perceptions that succeed one another with inconceivable rapidity. These bundles are constantly changing and in flux. We seem to have a natural propensity to imagine a *soul*, a *self*, or a *substance* that hides the discontinuity of these diverse experiences, but no such entity can be found. (This is the same argument as the Buddhist teaching that the skandhas are mistakenly imagined to be a self.)

CONTEMPORARY IDEALISTS

Idealism has really fallen out of fashion in Western philosophy, but there are contemporary thinkers who assert that the nature of reality is mental. I've already touched on panpsychism in previous sections, and some (but not all) panpsychists assert that the nature of all physical reality must be mental or experiential. These "pure" panpsychist theories are very different from the theories of Berkeley and Hume, but they might fit certain definitions of idealism.

It's hard to imagine what the underlying reality proposed by pan-psychist theories might be like. To the extent that you've tried to visualize how the inner nature of the physical could be mental, you've probably imagined that fundamental particles—photons, quarks, electrons, and other things that physics describes—are mind-stuff. That is what some panpsychist theories propose. However, there are also panpsychists who approach fundamental reality from a completely different angle. These approaches are known as *cosmopsychism*: the notion that a single cosmic entity is the underlying reality for all experience. Classically, this cosmic entity would be God. For contemporary theorists, it is the universe as a whole. This form of panpsychism goes hand in hand with contemporary theories of physics that challenge the notion of fundamental particles. The physicist David Tong writes,

> We learn in school that the basic building blocks of matter are particles. In fact, we often continue to teach this in universities where we explain that quarks and electrons form the Lego-bricks from which all matter is made.
>
> But this statement hides a deeper truth. According to our best laws of physics, the fundamental building blocks of Nature are not discrete particles at all. Instead they are continuous fluid-like substances, spread throughout all of space.[25]

Quantum field theory is generally considered to be the most successful current approach to particle physics, and weirdly enough, it views particles as ripples, or vibratory motions, in fields that temporarily appear as particles. Particles are not thought to be persistent things. Cosmopsychism asserts that the quantum field, as a whole, is mental or experiential. Instead of facing the combination problem of the micro-psychists, these theories face the challenge of explaining how this cosmic consciousness differentiates into the individual subjectivity that we each experience.

ARGUMENTS AGAINST IDEALISM

The general objection to idealism is this: if there is no material basis for our subjective experience, how can it be that the ocean tides always rise and fall with the rising and setting of the moon; how do the bare branches of winter predictably give rise to the soft green leaves of spring, the dark green leaves of summer, and eventually, the crimson and brown leaves of fall? The experiences are mental, but what underlies and causes them?

There are such strong structural relationships within experience that it is hard to imagine that there is nothing substantial that bears this structure. From everything we've been told by modern physics, the bearer of this structure is nothing like our commonsense view of matter. However, asserting that there is nothing at all goes against our deepest intuitions about the natural world. Proponents of idealism that assert that the stuff of the universe is exclusively mental and that matter is nonexistent, or an illusion, have a very steep hill to climb. They face as large an explanatory gap as the one faced by materialists.

WHERE THIS LEAVES US

David Chalmers concluded "Idealism and the Mind-Body Problem" with this assessment of the plausibility of various metaphysical positions:

> I do not claim that idealism is plausible. No position on the mind–body problem is plausible. Materialism is implausible. Dualism is implausible. Idealism is implausible. Neutral monism is implausible. None-of-the-above is implausible. But the probabilities of all of these views get a boost from the fact that one of them must be true. Idealism is not greatly less plausible than its main competitors. So even though idealism is implausible, there is a non-negligible probability that it is true.[26]

However intellectually unsatisfying this is, Chalmers's assessment of the state of play of contemporary philosophy rings true.

From my perspective, I think we should go with "none-of-the-above." I believe that none of the contemporary approaches to the hard problem gains traction because the problem is being approached from the wrong perspective—the perspective that mind and matter are *things* that are in some way related to each other. This seems to be fundamentally mistaken.

Again quoting Michel Bitbol:

This was well understood by Ludwig Wittgenstein, probably the most clear-headed philosopher of the twentieth century. One of my favorite quotes of Wittgenstein's is this one: "'[Conscious experience] is not a *something*, but not a *nothing* either!'" The fact that conscious experience is not some *thing*, that it is not a *thing* at all, makes it easy to forget, or tempting to neglect.[27]

————

What could be more ironic than thinking that mind is an illusion? That thought must occur to mind. If it's an illusion, it must be *a mental illusion.* As I believe we have seen, this is obvious to anyone who is not blinded by the assumption that everything must be physical. The mental domain is the domain of our experience. If you are having experience, you know for certain there is a mental domain.

The reality of the physical domain is not as easy to establish. Instinctively, we feel a material world must exist, but how can we be certain that there is anything underlying our experience? The only thing we have access to is experience. If there is a material world beyond our experience, it is not something we can ever encounter directly. We are always limited to inferences about what might under-lie experience, and these are always going to be merely mental models and conjectures.

From the perspective of a Buddhist practitioner, since liberation depends on directly recognizing the nature of mind, we don't need to worry too much about whether there's anything beyond mind. This might seem deeply disconcerting, but it is an excellent jumping-off point for the Mahayana journey. It reminds me of a quote attributed to Trungpa Rinpoche: "The bad news is you're falling through the air, nothing to hang on to, no parachute. The good news is, there's no ground."

APPENDIX 2

Root Text of the Seven Points of Training the Mind

TRANSLATED BY THE NALANDA TRANSLATION COMMITTEE

POINT ONE—THE PRELIMINARIES, WHICH ARE
A BASIS FOR DHARMA PRACTICE

I prostrate to the Great Compassionate One

1. First, train in the preliminaries.

POINT TWO—THE MAIN PRACTICE, WHICH IS
TRAINING IN BODHICHITTA

2. Regard all dharmas as dreams.
3. Examine the nature of unborn awareness.
4. Self-liberate even the antidote.
5. Rest in the nature of alaya, the essence.
6. In post-meditation, be a child of illusion.
7. Sending and taking should be practiced alternately.
    These two should ride the breath.
8. Three objects, three poisons, and three seeds of virtue.
9. In all activities, train with slogans.
10. Begin the sequence of sending and taking with yourself.

POINT THREE—TRANSFORMATION OF BAD
CIRCUMSTANCES INTO THE PATH OF ENLIGHTENMENT

11. When the world is filled with evil,
    Transform all mishaps into the path of bodhi.
12. Drive all blames into one.
13. Be grateful to everyone.
14. Seeing confusion as the four kayas
    Is unsurpassable shunyata protection.
15. Four practices are the best of methods.
16. Whatever you meet unexpectedly, join with meditation.

POINT FOUR—SHOWING THE UTILIZATION
OF PRACTICE IN ONE'S WHOLE LIFE

17. Practice the five strengths,
    The condensed heart instructions.
18. The Mahayana instruction for ejection of consciousness at
    death
    Is the five strengths: how you conduct yourself is important.

POINT FIVE—EVALUATION OF MIND TRAINING

19. All dharma agrees at one point.
20. Of the two witnesses, hold the principal one.
21. Always maintain only a joyful mind.
22. If you can practice even when distracted, you are well trained.

POINT SIX—DISCIPLINES OF MIND TRAINING

23. Always abide by the three basic principles.
24. Change your attitude, but remain natural.
25. Don't talk about injured limbs.
26. Don't ponder others.

27. Work with the greatest defilements first.
28. Abandon any hope of fruition.
29. Abandon poisonous food.
30. Don't be so predictable.
31. Don't malign others.
32. Don't wait in ambush.
33. Don't bring things to a painful point.
34. Don't transfer the ox's load to the cow.
35. Don't try to be the fastest.
36. Don't act with a twist.
37. Don't make gods into demons.
38. Don't seek others' pain as the limbs of your own happiness.

POINT SEVEN—GUIDELINES OF MIND TRAINING

39. All activities should be done with one intention.
40. Correct all wrongs with one intention.
41. Two activities: one at the beginning, one at the end.
42. Whichever of the two occurs, be patient.
43. Observe these two, even at the risk of your life.
44. Train in the three difficulties.
45. Take on the three principal causes.
46. Pay heed that the three never wane.
47. Keep the three inseparable.
48. Train without bias in all areas.
    It is crucial always to do this pervasively and wholeheartedly.
49. Always meditate on whatever provokes resentment.
50. Don't be swayed by external circumstances.
51. This time, practice the main points.
52. Don't misinterpret.
53. Don't vacillate.
54. Train wholeheartedly.
55. Liberate yourself by examining and analyzing.
56. Don't wallow in self-pity.

57. Don't be jealous.
58. Don't be frivolous.
59. Don't expect applause.

When the five dark ages occur,
This is the way to transform them into the path of the Bodhi.
This is the essence of the amrita of the oral instructions,
Which were handed down from the tradition of the sage of
    Suvarnadvipa.

Having awakened the karma of previous training
And being urged on by intense dedication,
I disregarded misfortune and slander
And received oral instruction on taming ego-fixation.
Now, even at death, I will have no regrets.

ACKNOWLEDGMENTS

My deepest gratitude goes to my root teachers: Shunryu Suzuki Roshi, whose *Zen Mind, Beginner's Mind* brought me onto the Mahayana path; Chögyam Trungpa Rinpoche, who adopted me after Suzuki Roshi's passing and nurtured me through spiritual adolescence; and Khenpo Tsültrim Gyamtso Rinpoche, who continued my training after Trungpa Rinpoche's parinirvana. All three of these extraordinary teachers have been present for me during the writing of this book.

Tsoknyi Rinpoche, Dzongsar Khyentse Rinpoche, Dzogchen Ponlop Rinpoche, Karl Brunnhölzl, John Dunne, Mindroling Khandro Rinpoche—each of these wonderful teachers and spiritual friends have been kind to me. They all contributed to the good qualities of this book, in both obvious and subtle ways.

For over a quarter of a century, I've worked with Barry Boyce on one dharma project after another. He is a dear friend, editor, mentor, and guardian. This is the third book we've done together. As editor and friend, he subdues what needs to be subdued, he uplifts what needs to be uplifted, and he destroys what needs to be destroyed. We have shared many a meal, gone for many a walk, done many a practice, and together shared many a joy and sorrow. Barry has never let me down. I could not ask for a better comrade in arms.

I have known and looked up to Matthieu Ricard for over forty years. I first met Matthieu when he was translating for Dilgo Khyentse Rinpoche in Paris in the 1980s. Since moving to Nova Scotia, I've mostly admired him from afar. When I thought about who might be able to write an authoritative foreword covering both Buddhism and Western philosophy, I thought Matthieu would be ideal. Yet with all his humanitarian and dharmic projects, I found it hard to imagine he would have time to do it. I am so grateful that he agreed—which he did with characteristic humility, humor, and charm.

I would never have started down the road of contemporary philosophy had I not stumbled upon the brilliant work of David Chalmers. By distinguishing the hard problem of consciousness from the easy problems, he went against the prevailing materialist ethos and showed that there must be a place for mind in the natural world. For me, his work creates space for the profound teachings of the Mahayana within a contemporary intellectual milieu that is generally infatuated with the material.

When I was struggling to find my way through various competing philosophical positions, my friend Jakob Leschly provided me with key insights I needed to move forward, introducing me to the work of Michel Bitbol. Likewise, when I was confused about early Yogachara presentations of the three natures, Jonathan Gold was kind enough to clarify Vasubandhu's view, unlocking a key feature of the Yogachara teachings. I'm grateful to both of them.

Many friends have been kind enough to take the time to read and comment on various versions of this manuscript. I am especially grateful to Larry Mermelstein, Yara Vrolijks, Michael Speraw, Scott Wellenbach, and Gina Mermelstein, who read early versions of this book and gave me invaluable suggestions for strengthening the structure, correcting mistakes, and making improvements.

Jim Lowrey, Tim Olmsted, Molly de Shong, Sid Rankaduwa, Luís Santiago Israel, Nancy Johnston, Ryan Jones, Marion Stork, Paddy McMullen, and Ken Friedman all read later versions of the manuscript and gave valuable feedback.

I am grateful to Dominique Side, Sébastien Reggiany, Astrid Hubert, Alain Beauregard, and Paul Brusa who kindly gave me opportunities to teach some of this material. Discussions with participants at these programs helped me learn effective ways to communicate these teachings.

I am very fortunate to have Shambhala as my publisher. In particular, I would like to thank Nikko Odiseos, Ivan Bercholz, Anna Wolcott Johnson, Casey Kemp, Samantha Ripley, Daniel Urban-Brown, Katrina Noble, and Natasha Kimmet, as well as the people who work behind the scenes. They all work with such professionalism, skill, and dedication to genuine dharma.

And finally, I'm so grateful for the people who deeply enrich and adorn my life: my wonderful wife, Lynn; my sons, Alden and Douglas; my daughter-in-law, Missy; my late daughter-in-law, Aimee, who is deeply missed; and my fantastic grandsons, Travis and Wesley, bringers of much needed love, chaos, and great joy.

NOTES

FOREWORD

1. Dilgo Khyentse Rinpoche, *The Heart Treasure of the Enlightened Ones: The Practice of View, Meditation, and Action*, trans. Padmakara Translation Group (Boston: Shambhala, 1993).

2. For an exhaustive analysis of the various materialistic and reductionist views on consciousness, see the work of Michel Bitbol: Michel Bitbol, *La conscience a-t-elle une origine?: Des neurosciences à la pleine conscience: une nouvelle approche de l'esprit* (Paris: Flammarion, 2014). A summary of Bitbol's perspective is given in Michel Bitbol, "Is Consciousness Primary?" *NeuroQuantology* 6, no. 1 (2008): 53–71.

3. Christof Koch, *Consciousness: Confessions of a Romantic Reductionist* (Cambridge: MIT Press, 2017). See also the discussion between the Fourteenth Dalai Lama, Christof Koch, and myself in session 4 of the Mind & Life XXVI dialogues "Mind, Brain and Matter," Mind and Life Institute, www.mindandlife.org /insight/mind-and-life-xxvi-session-4/, and the edited transcript of these dialogues in Wendy Hasenkamp and Janna R. White, eds., *The Monastery and the Microscope: Conversations with the Dalai Lama on Mind, Mindfulness, and the Nature of Reality* (New Haven: Yale University Press, 2017).

4. For an extended discussion, see Matthieu Ricard and Wolf Singer, *Beyond the Self: Conversations between Buddhism and Neuroscience* (Cambridge: MIT Press, 2017).

INTRODUCTION

1. Chögyam Trungpa, *The Sadhana of Mahamudra*, trans. Chögyam Trungpa and Richard Arthure (Halifax, NS: Nalanda Translation Committee, 1990), 5.

2. United Nations, "UN Report: Nature's Dangerous Decline 'Unprecedented'; Species Extinction Rates 'Accelerating,'" *Sustainable Development* (blog), May 6, 2019, www.un.org /sustainabledevelopment/blog/2019/05/nature-decline -unprecedented-report/.

3. Steven Johnson, "How Humanity Gave Itself an Extra Life," *New York Times*, April 27, 2021, www.nytimes.com/2021/04/27 /magazine/global-life-span.html?searchResultPosition=2.

4. Trungpa, *The Sadhana of Mahamudra*, 17.

5. Some readers may find the shift from the ordinary use of the term *materialism* to the philosophical use of the term unsettling. The point is that physicalism, consumerism, and psychological and spiritual materialism are a range of phenomena that share a common root: they are all ways of grasping and clinging to mental phenomena.

6. The Buddhist teachings are sometimes divided into various "vehicles" (*yana* in Sanskrit) for traveling the path based on the views and methods employed by their followers. One scheme describes three vehicles: the *Shravakayana* (the Vehicle of the Hearers), the *Pratyekabuddhayana* (the Vehicle of the Solitary Buddhas), and the Mahayana (the Great Vehicle). The first two of these are sometimes grouped together and referred to as the *Hinayana*, or the Lesser Vehicle, which might seem like a dismissive term. I prefer Foundational Vehicle, a more respectful way of distinguishing these schools from the Mahayana.

CHAPTER 1. FOUR TRUTHS FOR NOBLE BEINGS

1. Andreas Doctor, ed., *The Play in Full (Lalitavistara)*, trans.

Dharmachakra Translation Committee (New York: 84000: Translating the Words of the Buddha, 2016), 25.3.

2. This image comes from Gangteng Tulku Rinpoche by way of Karl Brunnhölzl: "The ground manifestations are immediately recognized for what they are—the ground's very own self-appearances or display—versus being misperceived as objects that are something other than the ground, which is the beginning of samsaric dualistic delusion. Gangteng Tulku Rinpoche compares this to the situation when humans and dogs look into a mirror: humans immediately recognize themselves, whereas dogs do not. Rather, they perceive their own reflection as being another dog and act accordingly." Karl Brunnhölzl, *A Lullaby to Awaken the Heart: The Aspiration Prayer of Samantabhadra and Its Tibetan Commentaries* (Somerville, MA: Wisdom, 2018), 345.

CHAPTER 2. THE THREE TRAININGS

1. Khenpo Tsültrim Gyamtso, Ari Goldfield, and Rose Taylor, *Stars of Wisdom: Analytical Meditation, Songs of Yogic Joy, and Prayers of Aspiration* (Boston: Shambhala, 2010), 66.
2. David Chadwick, *To Shine One Corner of the World: Moments with Shunryu Suzuki: Stories of a Zen Master Told by His Students* (New York: Broadway Books, 2001), 3.

CHAPTER 3. AWAKENING

1. Chögyam Trungpa and Carolyn Rose Gimian, *The Collected Works of Chögyam Trungpa*, vol. 2, The Path Is the Goal; Training the Mind; Glimpses of Abhidharma; Glimpses of Shunyata; Glimpses of Mahayana; Selected Writings (Boulder: Shambhala, 2010), 458.
2. Andreas Doctor, ed., *The Play in Full (Lalitavistara)*, trans. Dharmachakra Translation Committee (New York: 84000: Translating the Words of the Buddha, 2016), 18.25.

3. Andreas Doctor, ed., *The Play in Full*, 19.84.
4. Andreas Doctor, ed., *The Play in Full*, 21.1.
5. Andreas Doctor, ed., *The Play in Full*, 18.17–21ab.
6. Andreas Doctor, ed., *The Play in Full*, 21.133.
7. Chögyam Trungpa, "Teachers' Training Course" (unpublished transcript, 1972), 5.

CHAPTER 4. TEXTURES OF FEELINGS

1. Tsoknyi Rinpoche and Eric Swanson, *Open Heart, Open Mind: Awakening the Power of Essence Love* (New York: Harmony Books, 2012), 135.

CHAPTER 5. PERCEPTION AND CONCEPTION

1. John D. Dunne, "Toward an Understanding of Non-Dual Mindfulness," *Contemporary Buddhism* 12, no. 1 (2011): 78, https://doi.org/10.1080/14639947.2011.564820.
2. Shunryu Suzuki Roshi's elegant phrase. Shunryu Suzuki and Trudy Dixon, *Zen Mind, Beginner's Mind* (New York: Weatherhill, 1970), 21.

CHAPTER 6. EXORCISING EGO

1. Rimpoche Nawang Gehlek, Gini Alhadeff, and Mark Magill, *Good Life, Good Death: Tibetan Wisdom on Reincarnation* (New York: Riverhead Books, 2001), 101.
2. Shāntideva, *The Way of the Bodhisattva: A Translation of the Bodhicharyāvatāra*, trans. Padmakara Translation Group, 2nd ed., revised (Boston: Shambhala, 2006).
3. Shāntideva, *Way of the Bodhisattva*, 101, verse 8.129.
4. The Ninth Karmapa, Wangchuk Dorje, *The Karmapa's Middle Way: Feast for the Fortunate*, trans. Tyler Dewar, Nitartha Institute Series (Ithaca, NY: Snow Lion, 2008).

5. Ninth Karmapa, *Karmapa's Middle Way*, 335, verse 6.120.
6. Jatang Tsogdruk Rangdrol Shabkar, *The Flight of the Garuda*, trans. Erik Pema Kunsang, 3rd ed. (Kathmandu, Nepal: Rangjung Yeshe Publications, 1988), 23.

CHAPTER 7. THROUGH THE LOOKING GLASS

1. His Holiness the Dalai Lama, Tenzin Gyatso, *The Universe in a Single Atom: The Convergence of Science and Spirituality* (New York: Morgan Road Books, 2005), 11f.
2. Andy Karr, *Contemplating Reality: A Practitioner's Guide to the View in Indo-Tibetan Buddhism* (Boston: Shambhala, 2007).
3. There was a minor school of Indian materialists called the Charvakas or Lokayatas. Unlike contemporary materialists, they rejected cause and effect relationships and advocated hedonism. Charvakas occasionally appear in Buddhist texts as opponents who argue that things arise without causes.

CHAPTER 8. THE HARD PROBLEM

1. Thomas Nagel, "What Is It Like to Be a Bat?" *The Philosophical Review* 83, no. 4 (1974): 436.
2. NYU Center for Mind, Brain and Consciousness, "David Chalmers on the Hard Problem of Consciousness (Tucson 1994)," YouTube video, 26:35, accessed November 1, 2018, www.youtube.com/watch?v=_lWp-6hH_6g.
3. This debate has largely taken place in the world of Anglo-American analytic philosophy. There is another branch of modern philosophy, continental phenomenology, that tries to investigate first-person perspectives. These schools have such different interests and methods that they rarely speak across party lines. Rather than opposing each other like different baseball teams, they've became more like a baseball and a football team, each playing its own game. This image of the schools comes from Lawrence

Cahoone's course: "Rise of 20th-Century Philosophy—Pragmatism," The Modern Intellectual Tradition: From Descartes to Derrida (class lecture 17, The Teaching Company, 2010).

4. David J. Chalmers, "Facing Up to the Problem of Consciousness," *Journal of Consciousness Studies* 2, no. 3 (1995): 200–219.
5. Chalmers, "Facing Up to the Problem of Consciousness," 201.
6. Joseph Levine, "Materialism and Qualia: The Explanatory Gap," *Pacific Philosophical Quarterly* 64 (October 1983): 354–61.
7. For an overview of scientific attempts to explain consciousness, see section 9 of Robert Van Gulick, "Consciousness," *The Stanford Encyclopedia of Philosophy*, ed. Edward N. Zalta, last modified January 14, 2014, https://plato.stanford.edu/archives /win2021/entries/consciousness/.
8. David J. Chalmers, *The Character of Consciousness*, Philosophy of Mind Series (New York: Oxford University Press, 2010), 6.
9. Stephen Hawking recounts this anecdote in *A Brief History of Time*: A well-known scientist (some say it was Bertrand Russell) once gave a public lecture on astronomy. He described how the Earth orbits around the sun and how the sun, in turn, orbits around the centre of a vast collection of stars called our galaxy. At the end of the lecture, a little old lady at the back of the room got up and said: "What you have told us is rubbish. The world is really a flat plate supported on the back of a giant tortoise." The scientist gave a superior smile before replying, "What is the tortoise standing on?" "You're very clever, young man, very clever," said the old lady. "But it's turtles all the way down."
S. W. Hawking, *A Brief History of Time: From the Big Bang to Black Holes* (Toronto: Bantam Books, 1988), 2.

CHAPTER 9. ELIMINATIVE MATERIALISM

1. Galen Strawson, "A Hundred Years of Consciousness: 'A Long Training in Absurdity,'" *Estudios de Filosofía*, no. 59 (2019): 10.
2. Daniel Stoljar, "Physicalism," in *Stanford Encyclopedia of Philosophy*,

ed. Edward N. Zalta, February 13, 2001 (revised May 25, 2021), https://plato.stanford.edu/archives/win2017/entries/physicalism/.

3. William Ramsey, "Eliminative Materialism," in *Stanford Encyclopedia of Philosophy* (Summer 2020 ed.), ed. Edward N. Zalta, https://plato.stanford.edu/archives/sum2020/entries/materialism-eliminative.

4. Daniel C. Dennett, *Consciousness Explained* (Boston: Little, Brown, 1991), 33.

5. Daniel C. Dennett, "Facing Up to the Hard Question of Consciousness," *Philosophical Transactions of the Royal Society B: Biological Sciences* 373, no. 1755 (2018): 1, http://doi.org/10.1098/rstb.2017.0342.

6. Daniel C. Dennett, "Précis of Consciousness Explained," *Philosophy and Phenomenological Research* 53, no. 4 (1993): 891, https://doi.org/10.2307/2108259.

7. Dennett, "Précis of Consciousness Explained," 890.

8. This might seem far-fetched, but I'm not the only one to make such an observation. In a review of Dennett's *Sweet Dreams: Philosophical Obstacles to a Science of Consciousness*, philosopher Leslie Marsh wrote:
Dennett invokes Leibniz's factory metaphor: "a good theory of consciousness should make a conscious mind look like an abandoned factory, full of humming machinery and nobody home to supervise it, or enjoy it, or witness it." The "I" is neither something outside the physical world or something in addition to the team of busy, unconscious robots whose activities compose you; it should be included in the accounting by heterophenomenology. This loss of Self has strong resonance with Buddhist doctrine of annatta, no-self or no soul. This is the idea that the positing of a soul, a permanent and stable entity, is incoherent because all beings are subject to continuous change, death and decay. Beings are in a constant state of flux or "becoming." The human personality for annatta is an aggregate of several individual components.
Leslie Marsh, "Review [Reviewed Work: Sweet Dreams: Phil-

osophical Obstacles to a Science of Consciousness by Daniel C. Dennett]," *The Journal of Mind and Behavior* 26, no. 3 (2005): 209f.

CHAPTER 10. REDUCTIVE MATERIALISM

1. Michael Ruse, "Reductionism," in *The Oxford Companion to Philosophy*, ed. Ted Honderich 2nd ed. (Oxford University Press, 2005), 793.
2. J. J. C. Smart, "The Mind/Brain Identity Theory," in *Stanford Encyclopedia of Philosophy* (spring 2017 ed), ed. Edward N. Zalta, https://plato.stanford.edu/archives/spr2017/entries/mind-identity.

CHAPTER 11. THE CASE AGAINST MATERIALISM

1. Evan Thompson, *Waking, Dreaming, Being: Self and Consciousness in Neuroscience, Meditation, and Philosophy* (New York: Columbia University Press, 2015), XXXV.
2. Frank Jackson, "Epiphenomenal Qualia," *The Philosophical Quarterly* 32, no. 127 (April 1982): 127–36.
3. Jackson, "Epiphenomenal Qualia," 130.
4. Chalmers, *The Character of Consciousness*, 107.
5. Michel Bitbol, "Is Consciousness Primary?" *NeuroQuantology* 6, no. 1 (2008), doi:10.14704/nq.2008.6.1.157.
6. Bitbol, "Is Consciousness Primary?" 56.
7. Pico Iyer, "The Folly of the Weather Forecast," *Lion's Roar*, January 29, 2015, www.lionsroar.com/the-folly-of-the-weather-forecast-january-2011.

CHAPTER 12. TRACES OF THE BUDDHA

1. Jan Nattier, "The Heart Sutra: A Chinese Apocryphal Text?" *The Journal of the International Association of Buddhist Studies* 15, no. 2 (1992): 199.

2. Buddhavacana Translation Group, trans., *The Sūtra on Dependent Arising (Pratītyasamutpādasūtra)* (New York: 84000: Translating the Words of the Buddha, 2016), https://read.84000.co/translation/toh212.html.

3. Thānissaro Bhikku, "The Shorter Exhortation to Māluṅkya Cūḷa Māluṅkyovāda Sutta (MN 63)," accessed June 9, 2022, www.dhammatalks.org/suttas/MN/MN63.html.

4. Johannes Bronkhorst, *Buddhist Teaching in India*, Studies in Indian and Tibetan Buddhism (Boston: Wisdom, 2009), 63f.

5. Noa Ronkin, "Abhidharma," in *Stanford Encyclopedia of Philosophy* (summer 2018 ed.), ed. Edward N. Zalta, https://plato.stanford.edu/archives/sum2018/entries/abhidharma.

CHAPTER 13. THE MAHAYANA EMERGES

1. Paul Williams, Anthony Tribe, and Alexander Wynne, *Buddhist Thought: A Complete Introduction to the Indian Tradition*, 2nd ed. (London: Routledge, 2012), 76.

2. Karl Brunnhölzl, *Gone Beyond: The Prajnaparamita Sutras, the Ornament of Clear Realization, and Its Commentaries in the Tibetan Kagyü Tradition*, Tsadra Foundation Series (Ithaca, NY: Snow Lion, 2010), 35–36.

3. Williams, Tribe, and Wynne, *Buddhist Thought*, 71.

4. Chögyam Trungpa and Carolyn Rose Gimian, The Collected Works of Chögyam Trungpa, vol. 3, Cutting through Spiritual Materialism; The Myth of Freedom; The Heart of the Buddha; Selected Writings (Boulder: Shambhala, 2010), 18.

CHAPTER 14. THE MIDDLE WAY

1. John Dunne, "Mahayana Philosophical Schools of Buddhism," in *Encyclopedia of Religion*, 2nd ed., ed. L. Jones et al. (New York: Macmillan Reference, 2005), 1205.

CHAPTER 15. EXPERIENCING EMPTINESS

1. The Ninth Karmapa, Wangchuk Dorje, *The Karmapa's Middle Way: Feast for the Fortunate*, trans. Tyler Dewar, Nitartha Institute Series (Ithaca, NY: Snow Lion, 2008), 164.
2. Khenpo Tsültrim Gyamtso and Nagarjuna, *The Sun of Wisdom: Teachings on the Noble Nagarjuna's Fundamental Wisdom of the Middle Way*, trans. Ari Goldfield (Boston: Shambhala, 2002), 5.
3. Gyamtso and Nagarjuna, *Sun of Wisdom*, 13.
4. Gyamtso and Nagarjuna, *Sun of Wisdom*, 114.
5. Gyamtso and Nagarjuna, *Sun of Wisdom*, 115.
6. Shunryu Suzuki Roshi's elegant phrase. Shunryu Suzuki and Trudy Dixon, *Zen Mind, Beginner's Mind* (New York: Weatherhill, 1970), 105.

CHAPTER 16. TWO REALITIES

1. The Ninth Karmapa, Wangchuk Dorje, *The Karmapa's Middle Way: Feast for the Fortunate*, trans. Tyler Dewar, Nitartha Institute Series (Ithaca, NY: Snow Lion, 2008), 204, verse 6.23.
2. Donald S. Lopez, *The Madman's Middle Way: Reflections on Reality of the Tibetan Monk Gendun Chopel* (Chicago: University of Chicago Press, 2006), 47–48.
3. Lopez, *Madman's Middle Way*, 50.
4. Albert Einstein, "On the Method of Theoretical Physics," *Philosophy of Science* 1, no. 2 (April 1934), 164.
5. Niels Bohr, *Essays 1958–1962 on Atomic Physics and Human Knowledge*, The Philosophical Writings of Niels Bohr (Woodbridge, CT: Ox Bow Press, 1987), 10.

CHAPTER 17. ILLUSORY FORMS

1. Elizabeth M. Callahan, trans., *Two-Part Hevajra Tantra*, unpublished text: part 2, chapter 3, verse 36.

2. Khenpo Tsültrim Gyamtso and Nagarjuna, *The Sun of Wisdom: Teachings on the Noble Nagarjuna's Fundamental Wisdom of the Middle Way*, trans. Ari Goldfield (Boston: Shambhala, 2002), 53.

CHAPTER 18. TWO BROTHERS TAKE IT TO ANOTHER LEVEL

1. Khenpo Tsültrim Gyamtso, *Progressive Stages of Meditation on Emptiness*, trans. Shenpen Hookham (Oxford, UK: Longchen Foundation, 1988), 78.
2. Khenpo Tsültrim Gyamtso and Nagarjuna, *The Sun of Wisdom: Teachings on the Noble Nagarjuna's Fundamental Wisdom of the Middle Way*, trans. Ari Goldfield (Boston: Shambhala, 2002), 86.
3. Gyamtso and Nagarjuna, *Sun of Wisdom*, 41.
4. Richard King, "Early Yogacara and Its Relationship with the Madhyamaka School," *Philosophy East and West* 44, no. 4 (1994): 662.

CHAPTER 19. MERE-COGNIZANCE

1. Jonathan C. Gold, "Vasubandhu," in *Stanford Encyclopedia of Philosophy* (summer 2018 ed.), ed. Edward N. Zalta, https://plato.stanford.edu/archives/sum2018/entries/vasubandhu/.
2. Vasubandhu, *Twenty Verses*. This translation is an amalgamation of several translations, principally from Stefan Anacker, trans., *Seven Works of Vasubandhu, the Buddhist Psychological Doctor*, Religions of Asia Series (Delhi: Motilal Banarsidass, 1984) and Mark Siderits, *Buddhism as Philosophy: An Introduction*, Ashgate World Philosophies Series (Aldershot, England: Ashgate, 2007).
3. Vasubandhu, *Twenty Verses*, verse 1.
4. Vasubandhu, *Twenty Verses*, verse 2.
5. Vasubandhu, *Twenty Verses*, verse 3 and 4a.
6. Thomas Nagel, "What Is It Like to Be a Bat?" *The Philosophical Review* 83, no. 4 (1974): 438.

7. Vasubandhu, *Twenty Verses*, verse 6.
8. This is a very parochial reference. I grew up in New York, rooting first for the Yankees and later for the Mets. Please substitute your own choice of teams and championships.
9. Anacker, *Seven Works of Vasubandhu*, 3.
10. Chittamatra was never used as the name of a school in India. It was a Tibetan invention.
11. Karl Brunnhölzl, *A Compendium of the Mahāyāna: Asaṅgás Mahāyānasaṃgraha and Its Indian and Tibetan Commentaries*, vol. 1, Tsadra Foundation Series (Boulder: Snow Lion, 2018), 204.
12. Vasubandhu, *Thirty Verses*. This translation is also an amalgamation of several translations, principally from Ben Connelly, Wei-jen Teng, and Norman Fischer, *Inside Vasubandhu's Yogacara: A Practitioner's Guide*, Somerville, Massachusetts: Wisdom Publications, 2016 and "Vasubandhu's *Triṃśikā-kārikā*, 'Thirty Verses,'" a draft translation by Sāgaramati https://thebuddhistcentre.com/system/files/groups/files/thirty_verses_trans.pdf.
13. Vasubandhu, *Thirty Verses*, verses 26–28.

CHAPTER 20. NEW INSIGHTS INTO CONSCIOUSNESS

1. The Third Karmapa, Rangjung Dorje, and Jamgön Kongrul Lodrö Taye, *The Profound Inner Principles*, trans. Elizabeth M. Callahan, Tsadra Foundation Series (Boston: Snow Lion, 2014), 110f.
2. Donald D. Hoffman, *The Case against Reality: Why Evolution Hid the Truth from Our Eyes* (New York: W. W. Norton, 2019).
3. Francis Crick, *The Astonishing Hypothesis: The Scientific Search for the Soul* (New York: Scribner, Maxwell Macmillan International, 1994), 3.
4. Hoffman, *Case against Reality*, 42.
5. Karl Brunnhölzl, *A Compendium of the Mahāyāna: Asaṅgás Mahāyānasaṃgraha and Its Indian and Tibetan Commentaries*, vol. 1, Tsadra Foundation Series (Boulder: Snow Lion, 2018), 162.

6. Brunnhölzl, *Compendium of the Mahāyāna*, 158
7. Vasubandhu, *Thirty Verses*, verses 1, 2a.

CHAPTER 21. THREE NATURES

1. Mark Siderits, *Buddhism as Philosophy: An Introduction*, Ashgate World Philosophies Series (Aldershot, England: Ashgate, 2007), 175.
2. His Holiness the Dalai Lama, Tenzin Gyatso, Thupten Jinpa, and John D. Dunne, *Science and Philosophy in the Indian Buddhist Classics*, vol. 2, trans. Dechen Rochard (Somerville, MA: Wisdom, 2020), 32.
3. Recent translations of Vasubandhu's *Instruction on the Three Natures* can be found in Karl Brunnhölzl, *Straight from the Heart: Buddhist Pith Instructions* (Ithaca, NY: Snow Lion, 2007), 47–53, and Jonathan C. Gold, *Paving the Great Way: Vasubandhu's Unifying Buddhist Philosophy* (New York: Columbia University Press, 2015), 247f.
4. John Dunne, "Mahayana Philosophical Schools of Buddhism," in *Encyclopedia of Religion*, 2nd ed., ed. L. Jones et al. (New York: Macmillan Reference, 2005), 1211.
5. Jan Westerhoff, *The Golden Age of Indian Buddhist Philosophy*, Oxford History of Philosophy (Oxford: Oxford University Press, 2018), 179.
6. Karl Brunnhölzl, *A Compendium of the Mahāyāna: Asaṅga's Mahāyānasaṃgraha and Its Indian and Tibetan Commentaries*, vol. 1, Tsadra Foundation Series (Boulder: Snow Lion, 2018), 204.

CHAPTER 22. WE ARE ALL BUDDHAS (WITH STAINS)

1. Elizabeth M. Callahan, trans., *Two-Part Hevajra Tantra*, unpublished text: part 2, chapter 4, verse 69.
2. *Tathagata* is an epithet for the Buddha. It means one who has "thus gone" or "thus come." *Garbha* means "womb," "matrix," or "essence."

3. Karl Brunnhölzl, *When the Clouds Part: The Uttaratantra and Its Meditative Tradition as a Bridge between Sūtra and Tantra*, Tsadra Foundation Series (Boston: Snow Lion, 2014), 411.

4. Brunnhölzl, *When the Clouds Part*, 393f.

5. Saraha, *People's Doha*, verse 45, in Karl Brunnhölzl, personal communication, December 7, 2021.

6. In Mahayana literature, buddhas are often described in terms or two or three *kayas*, the Sanskrit term for body. The *dharmakaya* is the truth body, or the empty-luminous basic nature. When two bodies of a buddha are enumerated, the second is the *rupakaya*, or form body—the manifestations of this empty-luminosity (this includes both the *sambhogakaya* and the *nirmanakaya*). When three bodies are enumerated, they are the dharmakaya, the sambhogakaya (body of enjoyment), and the nirmanakaya ("emanation body," the one that is visible to other beings).

7. Brunnhölzl, *When the Clouds Part*, 365f.

CHAPTER 23. WHERE RUBBER AND ROAD MEET

1. Khenchen Thrangu, *The Seven Points of Mind Training*, Bibliotheca Indo-Buddhica Series, 1st Indian ed. (Delhi: Sri Satguru Publications, 2002), 5.

2. Patrul Rinpoche, *The Words of My Perfect Teacher*, 2nd ed. (Boston: Shambhala, 1998), 126.

3. Shambhala Publications has a list of these resources in "Lojong; Training the Mind," Mind Training Reader's Guide, accessed June 9, 2022, www.shambhala.com/lojong-mind-training.

4. Jamgon Kongtrul, *The Great Path of Awakening: The Classic Guide to Lojong, a Tibetan Buddhist Practice for Cultivating the Heart of Compassion*, trans. Kenneth J. McLeod (Boston: Shambhala, 2005), 31.

5. Kongtrul, *Great Path of Awakening*, 31.

6. Kongtrul, *Great Path of Awakening*, 32.

230 NOTES

CHAPTER 24. COMPASSION IN AN ILLUSORY WORLD

1. This piece was written during a peak of the COVID-19 pandemic.
2. Farhad Manjoo, "I Tried Microsoft's Flight Simulator. The Earth Never Seemed So Real," *New York Times*, August 19, 2020, www.nytimes.com/2020/08/19/opinion/microsoft-flight-simulator.html?action=click.
3. This point was made by Khenpo Tsültrim Gyamtso during a discussion with his students at Karmê Chöling.
4. Chögyam Trungpa, *The Collected Works of Chögyam Trungpa*, vol. 8, *Great Eastern Sun; Shambhala; Selected Writings* (Boulder: Shambhala, 2010), 241f.
5. The Editorial Board, "The Pope on Panhandling: Give without Worry," *New York Times*, March 3, 2017, www.nytimes.com/2017/03/03/opinion/the-pope-on-panhandling-give-without-worry.html.
6. Arne Naess, Alan R. Drengson, and Bill Devall, *Ecology of Wisdom: Writings by Arne Naess* (Berkeley: Counterpoint, 2008), 99.
7. Chögyam Trungpa and Carolyn Rose Gimian, *Shambhala: The Sacred Path of the Warrior* (Boston: Shambhala, 1984), 125.

CHAPTER 25. THE END

1. Chögyam Trungpa, "The Four Reminders," unpublished verse composed in English, 1974.
2. Adapted by the author from KM Ganguly, "Mahabharata Vana Parva - Translation by KM Ganguly," Mahabharata Online, www.mahabharataonline.com/translation/mahabharata_03311.php.
3. Dzogchen Ponlop, *Mind Beyond Death* (Ithaca, NY: Snow Lion, 2007), 9f.
4. Dzogchen Ponlop, *Mind Beyond Death*, 164.
5. Dzogchen Ponlop, *Mind Beyond Death*, 10.
6. Dzogchen Ponlop, *Mind Beyond Death*, 161.

APPENDIX 1: CONTEMPORARY THINKING
ABOUT MIND AND NATURE

1. Adam Becker, *What Is Real?: The Unfinished Quest for the Meaning of Quantum Physics* (New York: Basic Books, 2018), 5.
2. Scott Calef, "Dualism and Mind," in *Internet Encyclopedia of Philosophy*, www.iep.utm.edu/dualism/.
3. David Hume, *A Treatise of Human Nature: Being an Attempt to Introduce the Experimental Method of Reasoning into Moral Subjects and Dialogues Concerning Natural Religion* (London: Longmans, Green, 1878), 533.
4. Andrea Lavazza and Howard Robinson, eds., *Contemporary Dualism: A Defense*, Routledge Studies in Contemporary Philosophy (New York: Routledge, 2014), 5.
5. Galileo Galilei, *Discoveries and Opinions of Galileo*, trans. Stillman Drake (Garden City, NY: Doubleday, 1957), 53.
6. Becker, *What Is Real?*, 1f.
7. Bertrand Russell, *Portraits from Memory: And Other Essays* (New York: Simon and Schuster, 1956), 145.
8. Bertrand Russell, *An Outline of Philosophy* (London: G. Allen & Unwin, 1927), 139.
9. Russell, *Portraits from Memory*, 147.
10. Russell, *An Outline of Philosophy*, 306f.
11. Russell, *Portraits from Memory*, 164.
12. Ernst Mach, *Knowledge and Error: Sketches on the Psychology of Enquiry*, Vienna Circle Collection (Dordrecht, Holland: D. Reidel, 1976), 9.
13. Galen Strawson, "A Hundred Years of Consciousness: 'A Long Training in Absurdity,'" *Estudios de Filosofía*, no. 59 (2019): 12f.
14. Galen Strawson, "Realistic Monism: Why Physicalism Entails Panpsychism," in *Real Materialism: and Other Essays* (Oxford: Clarendon, 2008), 53.
15. Galen Strawson, "Consciousness Isn't a Mystery. It's Matter," *New York Times*, May 16, 2016, www.nytimes.com/2016/05/16/opinion/consciousness-isnt-a-mystery-its-matter.html.

16. Strawson, "Realistic Monism," 73.
17. Carl Zimmer, "Sizing Up Consciousness by Its Bits," *New York Times*, September 20, 2010, www.nytimes.com/2010/09/21/science/21consciousness.html.
18. Gary Marcus, "How Much Consciousness Does an iPhone Have?" *New Yorker*, June 19, 2017, www.newyorker.com/tech/annals-of-technology/how-much-consciousness-does-an-iphone-have.
19. Christof Koch, "A Theory of Consciousness," *Scientific American Mind* 20, no. 4 (2009): 16–19.
20. David Chalmers, "Idealism and the Mind-Body Problem," in *The Routledge Handbook of Panpsychism*, ed. William E. Seager (New York: Routledge, 2020), 353.
21. George Berkeley, *Principles of Human Knowledge* and *Three Dialogues*, ed. Howard Robinson, World's Classics (Oxford: Oxford University Press, 1996), 38.
22. Berkeley, *Principles*, 25.
23. Berkeley, *Principles*, 27.
24. Berkeley, *Principles*, 32.
25. David Tong, "What Is Quantum Field Theory?" Department of Applied Mathematics and Theoretical Physics, University of Cambridge, accessed June 9, 2022, www.damtp.cam.ac.uk/user/tong/whatisqft.html.
26. Chalmers, "Idealism and the Mind-Body Problem," 370.
27. The quote from Ludwig Wittgenstein's *Philosophical Investigations* is found in Michel Bitbol and Olafur Eliasson, *Never Known, but Is the Knower / Jamais connu, il est le connaissant* (Berlin: Institut für Raumexperimente, 2014), 5.

SELECTED BIBLIOGRAPHY

This bibliography contains a selection of resources for further study. It lists the major works consulted in the preparation of this book. If you are looking for additional reference material about specific citations, please refer to the endnotes.

Becker, Adam. *What Is Real?: The Unfinished Quest for the Meaning of Quantum Physics*. New York: Basic Books, 2018.

Berkeley, George. *Principles of Human Knowledge* and *Three Dialogues*. Edited by Howard Robinson. World's Classics. Oxford: Oxford University Press, 1996.

Bronkhorst, Johannes. *Buddhist Teaching in India*. Studies in Indian and Tibetan Buddhism. Boston: Wisdom, 2009.

Brunnhölzl, Karl. *A Compendium of the Mahāyāna: Asaṅga's Mahāyānasaṃgraha and Its Indian and Tibetan Commentaries*. 3 vols. Tsadra Foundation Series. Boulder: Snow Lion, 2018.

———. *Gone Beyond: The Prajnaparamita Sutras, the Ornament of Clear Realization, and Its Commentaries in the Tibetan Kagyü Tradition*. Tsadra Foundation Series. Ithaca, NY: Snow Lion, 2010.

———. *A Lullaby to Awaken the Heart: The Aspiration Prayer of Samantabhadra and Its Tibetan Commentaries*. Somerville, MA: Wisdom, 2018.

———. *Straight from the Heart: Buddhist Pith Instructions*. Ithaca, NY: Snow Lion, 2007.

———. *When the Clouds Part: The Uttaratantra and Its Meditative Tradition as a Bridge between Sūtra and Tantra*. Tsadra Foundation Series. Boston: Snow Lion, 2014.

Chadwick, David. *To Shine One Corner of the World: Moments with Shunryu Suzuki: Stories of a Zen Master Told by His Students.* New York: Broadway Books, 2001.

Chalmers, David J. *The Character of Consciousness.* Philosophy of Mind Series. New York: Oxford University Press, 2010.

———. *The Conscious Mind: In Search of a Fundamental Theory.* Philosophy of Mind Series. New York: Oxford University Press, 1996.

———. "Facing Up to the Problem of Consciousness." *Journal of Consciousness Studies* 2, no. 3 (1995): 200–219.

Dennett, D. C. *Consciousness Explained.* Boston: Little Brown, 1991.

Descartes, René, John Cottingham, and Bernard Williams. *Meditations on First Philosophy: With Selections from the Objections and Replies.* Cambridge Texts in the History of Philosophy. 2nd ed. Cambridge: Cambridge University Press, 2017.

Galilei, Galileo. *Discoveries and Opinions of Galileo.* Translated by Stillman Drake. New York: Anchor Books, 1957.

Gold, Jonathan C. *Paving the Great Way: Vasubandhu's Unifying Buddhist Philosophy.* New York: Columbia University Press, 2015.

Gyamtso, Khenpo Tsültrim. *The Presentation of the Classifications of Mental States Called the Essence of the Ocean of Texts on Reasoning.* Translated and edited by Karl Brunnhölzl. Duncan, B.C., Canada: Nitartha Institute, 2003.

Gyamtso, Khenpo Tsültrim, Ari Goldfield, and Rose Taylor. *Stars of Wisdom: Analytical Meditation, Songs of Yogic Joy, and Prayers of Aspiration.* Boston: Shambhala, 2010.

Gyamtso, Khenpo Tsültrim, and Shenpen Hookham. *Progressive Stages of Meditation on Emptiness.* Translated by Shenpen Hookham. Oxford: Longchen Foundation, 1988.

Gyamtso, Khenpo Tsültrim, and Nagarjuna. *The Sun of Wisdom: Teachings on the Noble Nagarjuna's Fundamental Wisdom of the Middle Way.* Translated by Ari Goldfield. Boston: Shambhala, 2002.

His Holiness the Dalai Lama, Tenzin Gyatso. *The Universe in a Single Atom: The Convergence of Science and Spirituality.* New York: Morgan Road Books, 2005.

His Holiness the Dalai Lama, Tenzin Gyatso, Thupten Jinpa, and
John D. Dunne. *Science and Philosophy in the Indian Buddhist
Classics*. Vol. 2, translated by Dechen Rochard. Somerville, MA:
Wisdom, 2020.

Hoffman, Donald D. *The Case against Reality: Why Evolution Hid the
Truth from Our Eyes*. New York: W. W. Norton, 2019.

Hume, David. *A Treatise of Human Nature: Being an Attempt to Introduce
the Experimental Method of Reasoning into Moral Subjects and Dialogues Concerning Natural Religion*. London: Longmans, Green, 1878.

Jones, Lindsay, Mircea Eliade, and Charles J. Adams. *Encyclopedia of
Religion*. 2nd ed. 15 vols. Detroit: Macmillan Reference USA, 2005.

Karr, Andy. *Contemplating Reality: A Practitioner's Guide to the View
in Indo-Tibetan Buddhism*. Boston: Shambhala, 2007.

Kongtrul, Jamgon. *The Great Path of Awakening: The Classic Guide
to Lojong, a Tibetan Buddhist Practice for Cultivating the Heart of
Compassion*. Translated by Kenneth J. McLeod. Boston: Shambhala, 2005.

Lavazza, Andrea, and Howard Robinson, eds. *Contemporary Dualism: A Defense*. Routledge Studies in Contemporary Philosophy.
New York: Routledge, 2014.

Levine, Joseph. "Materialism and Qualia: The Explanatory Gap."
Pacific Philosophical Quarterly 64 (October 1983): 354–61.

Lopez Jr., Donald S. *The Madman's Middle Way: Reflections on Reality
of the Tibetan Monk Gendun Chopel*. Chicago: University of Chicago Press, 2006.

Mach, Ernst. *Knowledge and Error: Sketches on the Psychology of
Enquiry*. Vienna Circle Collection. Dordrecht, Holland: D.
Reidel, 1976.

Nagel, Thomas. *Mind and Cosmos: Why the Materialist Neo-
Darwinian Conception of Nature Is Almost Certainly False*. New
York: Oxford University Press, 2012.

Nattier, Jan. "The Heart Sutra: A Chinese Apocryphal Text?" *The
Journal of the International Association of Buddhist Studies* 15, no. 2
(1992): 199.

Ponlop, Dzogchen. *Mind Beyond Death*. Ithaca, NY: Snow Lion, 2007.

Russell, Bertrand. *An Outline of Philosophy*. London: G. Allen & Unwin, 1927.

———. *Portraits from Memory: And Other Essays*. New York: Simon and Schuster, 1956.

Seager, W. E. *The Routledge Handbook of Panpsychism*. New York: Taylor & Francis, 2019.

Shabkar, Jatang Tsogdruk Rangdrol. *The Flight of the Garuda*. Translated by Erik Pema Kunsang. 3rd ed. Kathmandu, Nepal: Rangjung Yeshe Publications, 1988.

Shāntideva. *The Way of the Bodhisattva: A Translation of the Bodhich-aryāvatāra*. Translated by the Padmakara Translation Group. 2nd ed., revised. Boston: Shambhala, 2006.

Siderits, Mark. *Buddhism as Philosophy: An Introduction*. Ashgate World Philosophies Series. Aldershot, England: Ashgate, 2007.

Stoljar, Daniel. "Physicalism." In *Stanford Encyclopedia of Philoso-phy*, edited by Edward N. Zalta. February 13, 2001; revised May 25, 2021. https://plato.stanford.edu/archives/win2017/entries/physicalism.

Suzuki, Shunryu, and Trudy Dixon. *Zen Mind, Beginner's Mind*. New York: Weatherhill, 1970.

The Third Karmapa, Rangjung Dorje, and Jamgön Kongrul Lodrö Taye. *The Profound Inner Principles*. Translated by Elizabeth M. Callahan. Tsadra Foundation Series. Boston: Snow Lion, 2014.

Thompson, Evan. *Waking, Dreaming, Being: Self and Consciousness in Neuroscience, Meditation, and Philosophy*. New York: Columbia University Press, 2015.

Thrangu, Khenchen. *The Seven Points of Mind Training*. Bibliotheca Indo-Buddhica Series. 1st Indian ed. Delhi: Sri Satguru Publica-tions, 2002.

Trungpa, Chögyam. *Cutting through Spiritual Materialism*. Clear Light Series. Berkeley: Shambhala, 1973.

———. *The Sadhana of Mahamudra*. Translated by Chögyam Trungpa and Richard Arthure. Halifax, NS: Nalanda Translation Committee, 1990.

Trungpa, Chögyam, and Carolyn Rose Gimian. *The Collected Works of Chögyam Trungpa*. Vol. 2, *The Path Is the Goal; Training the Mind; Glimpses of Abhidharma; Glimpses of Shunyata; Glimpses of Mahayana; Selected Writings*. Boulder: Shambhala, 2010.

———. *The Collected Works of Chögyam Trungpa*. Vol. 3, *Cutting through Spiritual Materialism; the Myth of Freedom; the Heart of the Buddha; Selected Writings*. Boulder: Shambhala, 2010.

———. *The Collected Works of Chögyam Trungpa*. Vol. 8, *Great Eastern Sun; Shambhala; Selected Writings*. Boulder: Shambhala, 2010.

———. *Shambhala: The Sacred Path of the Warrior*. Boston: Shambhala, 1984.

Tsoknyi Rinpoche, and Eric Swanson. *Open Heart, Open Mind: Awakening the Power of Essence Love*. New York: Harmony Books, 2012.

Vasubandhu, and Stefan Anacker. *Seven Works of Vasubandhu: the Buddhist Psychological Doctor*. Translated by Stefan Anacker. Religions of Asia Series. Delhi: Motilal Banarsidass, 1984.

Westerhoff, Jan. *The Golden Age of Indian Buddhist Philosophy*. Oxford History of Philosophy. Oxford: Oxford University Press, 2018.

Williams, Paul, Anthony Tribe, and Alexander Wynne. *Buddhist Thought: A Complete Introduction to the Indian Tradition*. 2nd ed. London: Routledge, 2012.

INDEX

death (*continued*)
  five strengths for, 168, 169, 210
  materialistic and theistic views of,
    179–80
  as opportunity, 184–85
  preparing for, 178
  suffering of, 14, 15
Deep Ecology movement, 176
Deer Park, 3, 99
defilements. *See* kleshas (afflictions)
definitive teachings, 97
deities
  in bardo, 184
  Mahayana understanding of, 127
delusion, 6, 9, 17, 49, 69, 121, 125, 151
Dennett, Daniel, xi, 60–63
dependent arising, 86, 113
  of appearances, 100–101, 106, 110,
    111, 145
  conventional truth as, 116–17
  doctrinal unanimity of, 129
  and emptiness, inseparability of,
    173–74
  popular and Madhyamaka
    understandings of, difference
    between, 101
  time and, 140
Descartes, René, 189–90, 191. *See also*
  under dualism
desire, 15, 16, 89, 127, 145, 158, 186
desire realm, 15
dharma theory, 72, 89, 92, 125, 140–41
dharmakaya, 160, 161, 180
discursiveness, 23–24, 25, 28, 31–32
disintegrating collections. *See*
  skandhas
dissatisfaction, 3, 4–5, 158
distraction, 19
  in daily life, 23–24
  as ego's resistance, 40
  in meditation, 20, 32, 40, 120–21
doubt, 16, 41–42
dreams, 97
  as example, 122, 133, 135
  memory and, 152
  projections as, 5, 18, 172
  regarding all dharmas as, 165, 209

dualism, 188–89, 201, 206
  Cartesian, 48, 130, 189–90
  eliminative view of, 60–61
  objections to, 189, 191
  property, 190
  sensation of, 146
  Yogachara view of, 147, 148
Dunne, John, 28, 96, 148–49

ego, 34
  ethical conduct and, 9
  harm caused by, 36–37
  in neutral monism, 196
  reinforcing itself, 125
  reproaching, 169
  resistance from, 40
  self-criticism and, 18
  self-deception of, 35, 163
  as superimposition, 36
  taming, 41, 170
ego-clinging, 6, 125, 168
eight consciousnesses, 144–46, 148,
  149. *See also* alaya consciousness
eightfold path, 98, 99. *See also* path:
  truth of
Einstein, Albert, 117–18, 192, 193
eliminativism, xi, 60–61, 64
emotional veils, 6, 9, 10, 11
emotions, 16–17
  in bardo, 184
  death and, 178, 182
  illusory forms practice and, 121
  investigating, 56
  nature of, recognizing, 49
  painful, looking directly at, 32–33
  self and, 35–36
  in shamatha, 11, 20
  symbols of, 127
empathy, 49, 166
empiricism, 202
emptiness (*shunyata*), 92, 93, 98, 99,
  112, 210
  and appearance, union of, 111, 122
  and compassion, inseparability
    of, 173
  concepts of, abandoning, 125–26,
    137

as dependent arising, 101
direct experience of, 102
doctrinal unanimity of, 129
as mere negation, 124
Middle Way view of, 100, 113
of persons, 114
purpose of experiencing, 110–11
Entrance to the Middle Way (Chandrakirti), 37
environment, xv, 175–76
envy, true nature of, 127
"Epiphenomenal Qualia" (Jackson),
71–72
equalizing oneself for others, 162, 173
eternalism, 100, 180
ethical conduct (*shila*), 7–10
everyday life
    dharma practice in, 163, 168–69,
        172–73, 210
    discursiveness in, 31–32
    feelings in, working with, 26
    illusory nature of, 121–23
existence
    clinging to, 126
    of dharmas, 125
    eternalism and, 100
    experience and, xix, 197
    idealist views of, 202, 203, 204
    independent, 130
    materialist view of, 69
    Nagarjuna's reasonings on, 103–5
    Yogachara view of, 150–51
experience, 77
    abstraction of, 74–75
    arising of, 54
    death and, 179
    in dharma theory, 89
    in dharma transmission, 94–95
    distrusting, 75
    idealism and, 206
    in Integrated Information Theory,
        200
    mental domain of, 207
    in neutral monism, 195–96
    in real physicalism, 197
    reductionism and, 68
    reifying, 172

scientific theory and, 117–18
subjectivity of, 57
three aspects of (conventional),
    195
Yogachara understanding of,
    131–32
explanatory gap, 55–57, 71, 76
    Berkeley on, 203–4
    combination problem and, 199
    dualism and, 191
    idealism and, 206
    reductionist approaches to, 66,
        67–68

"Facing Up to the Problem of Con-
    sciousness" (Chalmers), 53–54
faith, 8, 67, 116
faults, hidden, 163
fear, 16, 69
    of feelings, 23–25
    resting within, 11
    subconscious, 5
    welcoming, 18
    See also hope and fear
feelings
    contemporary attitudes toward,
        22–23
    directly encountering, 24–25
    nature of, recognizing, 49
    as self, investigating, 35–36, 39
    skandha of, 109
    suppressing, 23–23
    three natures and, 152
    working with, 25–27
First [Buddhist] Council, 85
first-person perspectives, 57, 62,
    67–68, 72, 178
five strengths, 168–69, 210
Five Treatises of Maitreya, 156. See also
    Uttaratantra (*Treatise on the Supreme
    Continuum of the Mahayana*)
five wisdoms, 127
"Flower Sermon," 84
"Folly of the Weather Forecast, The"
    (Iyer), 76–77
Foundational Vehicle, xviii, 5, 9, 10
four marks, 98

suffering of, 5
  in wishing happiness for others, 37

karma, 86, 177
  appearances and, 135–36
  cutting through, 168
  overcoming, 169–70
Kashmir, 127–28
kindness, 170
King, Richard, 128–29
kleshas (afflictions), 86, 145, 156, 158, 169–70, 211
knowledge argument, 71–72, 76
knowledge veils, 6, 10, 11
Koch, Christof, 200, 201
Kongtrul, Jamgön, 139–40

Lalitavistara (The Play in Full), 14, 16, 19
language, conventions of, 116
latent tendencies, 141
  at death, 180
  dharmakaya as free from, 161
  of ignorance, 172
  maturation of, 146
  Yogachara view of, 144, 148, 151
Lavazza, Andrea, 191
liberation, 49, 149, 208
  within, 83, 97
  as Buddha's central concern, 85
  longing for, 185
  potential for, 159
Locke, John, 72
logic, 40, 100. See also reasoning
lojong. See mind training (lojong)
love, 8, 23, 162, 188
luminosity, 17, 182–83
luminous-emptiness, 10, 166, 168, 172

Mach, Ernst, 194
Madhyamaka (Middle Way) tradition, 99–101, 124, 131
  absolute reality in, 113
  emptiness in, 125, 126
  focus of, 141
  and Yogachara, relationship between, 128–29, 137

Mahabharata, 177–78
Mahayana, 96, 185
  abhidharma's effect on, 90, 92
  antecedents of, 84
  Asanga's influence on, 126–27
  on cause of suffering, 5
  central concerns of, 36
  conduct of, 9–10
  contributions of, 93
  on death, 180
  on independent existence, 130
  Nagarjuna's influence on, 99
  origins of, 68–69, 93–94
  polemics in, 136–37
  progressive stages of, xix
  Vasubandhu's conversion to, 128
  wisdom in, xviii
Maitreya, 127, 155–56. See also Five Treatises of Maitreya
Malunkyaputta, 85
Manjoo, Farhad, 171–72
Mara, 15–17
materialism, 59–60, 176, 188, 201, 206
  clinging to, 69
  as conception, 76
  in contemporary culture, xvii–xviii
  death and, 179
  hidden beliefs in, 50
  as primary reality, 73
  scientific, 47, 74, 191
  three lords of, xvi–xvii
  See also eliminativism; physicalism; reductionism
mathematics, 74, 192–93, 198
matter, 189
  contemporary assumptions about, xix, 47
  in cosmopsychism, 205
  in idealism, 202, 206
  as limited to inference, 207
  in real physicalism, 197–98
  scientific view, evolution of, 191–93
meditation, 7, 86
  in abhidharma tradition, 89
  beginning, 32

objects
  Berkeley's view of, 203
  as dependently arisen appear-
    ances, 110
  false constructions of, 147
  formation of, 139
  Yogachara view of, 133, 150–51
obscurations, two types, 6, 156. *See also*
  emotional veils; knowledge veils
obstacles
  clinging, 125
  transforming into path, 49,
    167–68, 210
Occam's Razor, 66
old age, suffering of, 14, 15
oppression and inequality, 175–76
oral tradition, 84, 88

Padmasambhava, 180
pain, 33, 65, 68
panpsychism, 188, 194, 196, 201
  idealism and, 204–5
  objections to, 198–200
  See also cosmopsychism; Inte-
    grated Information Theory
    (IIT); neutral monism; real
    physicalism
paramita practices, 9–10, 92, 98
parinirvana, 85
path
  measuring progress on, 169–70,
    210
  transforming bad circumstances
    into, 167–68, 210
  truth of, 7, 12, 87, 98, 99
perception, 75, 143
  Berkeley's view of, 203
  common sense and, 131–32
  and conceptions, distinguishing
    between, 30–31, 32, 36, 195
  at death, 182
  experience and, 54
  extramental objects and, 135
  Hume's view of, 190, 204
  mistaken, 115
  subtly of, 29
  See also pure perception

permanence, 160–61
phenomena, 6, 12, 92, 110–11, 180. *See*
  also mental phenomena
phenomenal concept strategy, 67–68
phenomenology, 62
philosophy, 38, 96
  Buddhist, contemplative practices
    and, 96
  Buddhist view of, 151
  contemporary, purpose of under-
    standing, 187–88
  materialist, challenges to, 50–51
physicalism, xvii, 59–60, 71–72, 188.
  See also real physicalism
physics, xvii, 47, 55, 60, 192–93
  cosmopsychism and, 205
  and experience, relationship
    between, 117–18
  real physicalism and, 197–98
  reductionism in, 65
  See also quantum physics
Plato, 58
pleasure, ix, 5, 37, 190
Ponlop Rinpoche. See *Mind Beyond*
  Death
post-meditation, 209
posture, 18, 19–20
prajna. *See* wisdom
Prajnaparamita sutras, 92–93, 98, 99
preliminaries, 165, 209
pride, 125, 127
projections, xvii, 33, 120, 169, 174
  believing in, 121
  clinging to, 69
  craving and attachment as, 5
  emptiness of, 111
  as illusory, 172, 175
  knowledge veils and, 6
  onto inner experience, 36
  recognizing, 17, 18, 19
  in tonglen, 167
  Yogachara view of, 148
provisional teachings, 97, 98
psychology, 38, 47, 195–96
pure perception, 10, 122. *See also* illusory forms practices
purity, paramita of, 160–61

qualia inversion, 72–73
quantum field theory, 199, 205
quantum mechanics, 55
quantum physics, 189, 193, 196

Rangjung Dorje, Third Karmapa, 139–40
Ratnasambhava, 127
real physicalism, 197–98
reasoning, 117
    on coming and going, 106–8
    illustrations of (four-point), 105–6
    Nagarjuna's four-point reasoning, 103–5
    purpose of, 110
rebirth/reincarnation, 179–80, 181, 184, 185
reductionism, 64–65, 201
    approaches of, various, 65–67
    objections to, 50–51, 52, 67–68
    as philosophy not science, 47
reference points, 10, 34–35, 62, 161, 183
relative bodhichitta, 9, 166, 168, 169–70
relative truth, 111, 113. *See also* conventional reality
representationalist theories, 28, 66–67, 148–49, 203
Robinson, Howard, 191
Ronkin, Noa, 89
Russell, Bertrand, 193, 194, 195–96

samadhi of illusion, 122–23
samsara, 17, 69
    bondage in, 86
    buddha nature and, 158–59
    causes of, 160
    and nirvana, inseparability of, 98, 161
    suffering of, 177
San Francisco Zen Center, 19
Saraha, 160
Sarvastivada school, 140–41
Sautrantika school, 128, 141, 144
science and technology, xv–xvi, 77
    on consciousness, 70

dominance of, 48–49, 50
on meditation, 12
on mental domain, 58
as mere conventions, 117
naturalistic approach of, 67
on subjectivity, 55
sectarianism, 94
self (sense of "I")
    alaya mistaken as, 145
    clinging/grasping, 35, 138
    contemporary views of, 190
    illusory nature of, 63, 110
    instinctive and conditioned views of, 37–38
    investigating, 38–40, 180
    Nagarjuna's reasonings on, 108–9
    in neutral monism, 195
    paramita of, 160–61
    preserving through meditation, 22
    as projection, 5
    subtle, 147
    three natures and, 152
    transcending, 185
self-centeredness, 6, 164, 169
self-cherishing, 6, 9, 167
self-clinging, 8, 9, 148
self-concern, 34–35
self-deception, 35, 163, 170
selflessness, 38, 98, 195
    certainty in, 41
    Dennett on, 62–63
    doctrinal unanimity of, 129
    glimpsing, 40
    recognizing, 108
self-liberation, 159–60
self-mortification, 15, 18
self-nature (*svabhava*), 130
sense perception, 29, 31, 36, 108, 121
sensory experience, 56–57, 144, 148, 202, 203
Seven Points of Training the Mind, The, 163
    study aids, 164
    translation, 209–12
Seven Works on Vasubandhu (Anacker), 136–37

Shakyamuni Buddha, 3
    enlightenment journey of, 14–17
    as example, 83
    pragmatism of, 85–87, 140
    realization of, 6
shamatha (calm abiding), 11, 32, 39,
    165–66
Shantideva, 36–37
Shorter Discourse to Malunkyaputta,
    The, 85–87
shunyata. See emptiness (shunyata)
sickness, 14, 15, 23, 24, 166, 181
Siderits, Mark, 147
skandhas
    Dennett's Multiple Drafts theory
        and, 63
    description of, 108–9
    as self, 37, 41, 109–10, 204
Smart, J. J. C., 65
souls, 179–80, 190, 204
spacetime, 192–93
spiritual teachers, 163
Sri Lanka, 91
stains, incidental/adventitious, 97, 155,
    156, 157, 158, 159–60
Stoljar, Daniel, 67–68
Strawson, Galen, 59, 197–98, 199
subjectivity, 63
    eliminative views on, 61
    experience and, 57
    in panpsychism, 194–95
    in quantum field theory, 205
    reductionist views on, 64
    understanding, 53, 54–55
    Yogachara view of, 145, 148–49
subtle body, 22, 24, 26–27
suchness, 111, 138, 157
suffering, 4–5
    causes of, 86, 111
    extinguishing, 49, 50, 96
    mark of, 98
    meditation in eliminating, 12
    origin of (second truth), 5, 69
    of others, 167, 172–73, 174–75, 211
    three great domains of, 175–76
    transforming, 6
superimpositions, 29–30, 31, 36, 147

Sutra on Dependent Arising, 83–84
sutras, 84, 88, 92
Suvarnadvipa, 212
Suzuki Roshi, Shunryu, 10, 19, 110

Tathagatagarbha sutras, 98
Tenzin Gyatso, Fourteenth Dalai
    Lama, 47
theism, 179–80
Theravadin tradition, 84, 91
third-person perspectives, 49, 53, 62,
    68, 178, 179
Thirty Verses (Vasubandhu), 137–38,
    145–46
Thompson, Evan, 70
thoughts, 18, 28, 113
    chain reactions of, 111
    at death, 182
    investigating, 56
    in meditation, 11, 20, 21
    nature of, recognizing, 49
    perception and concept blended
        in, 29–30
    self and, 35–36
Thrangu Rinpoche, 162
"Three Great Movements, The"
    (Naess), 176
three marks of existence, 87
three natures, 149–50
    insight into, 153–54
    instructions on method, 151–53
    purpose of, 150
three turnings of dharma wheel,
    97–98, 99
Tibetan Book of the Dead, The. See
    Great Liberation Through Hearing in
    the Bardo, The
Tibetan Buddhism, 84, 136
time, 107, 116, 140–41, 192
Tong, David, 205
tonglen (sending and taking), 166–67,
    209
Tononi, Giulio, 200, 201
Treasury of the Abhidharma (Abhidhar-
    makosha, Vasubandhu), 128
Treatise Concerning the Principles of
    Human Knowledge, A (Berkeley), 202

Treatise of Human Nature, A (Hume), 190, 204
tripitaka "three baskets." *See* Buddhism: canons of
Trungpa, Chögyam, xv, 19, 112, 113, 164, 208
    on ecology and healing, 176
    on materialism, xvi
    on meditation, 14, 21
    on suffering of others, 174
    See also *Cutting Through Spiritual Materialism*; "Four Reminders, The"
Twenty Verses (Vasubandhu), 132, 133, 135
two realities, 113–14. *See also* conventional reality; ultimate truth
Two-Part Hevajra Tantra, 119

ultimate bodhichitta. *See* absolute bodhichitta
ultimate truth, 113. *See also* absolute reality
Upali, 85
Uttaratantra (*Treatise on the Supreme Continuum of the Mahayana*), 156, 157, 158, 160–61

Vaibhashika school, 128, 140
Vairochana, 127
Vasubandhu, 129, 147
    biographical information, 127–28
    system of, 130, 131, 136
    See also *Instruction on the Three Natures*; *Thirty Verses*; *Treasury of the Abhidharma* (*Abhidharmakosha*); *Twenty Verses*

view of transitory collection, 37
Vinaya, 85, 88, 93
vipashyana (clear seeing, insight), 11, 39, 165–66
virtue, 86, 99, 169, 170
vitalism, 61

Wangchuk Dorje, Ninth Karmapa, 102
warfare, 175–76
Way of the Bodhisattva, The (Shantideva), 36–37
Westerhoff, Jan, 150–51
Williams, Paul, 91, 93–94
wisdom, xviii, 49, 180, 183
    absolute reality and, 113
    bodhichitta and, 164, 165
    experience as expressing, 10
    gradual cultivation of, 12–13
    prajna, translations of, 7
    Shakyamuni's, 17
    See also five wisdoms
Wittgenstein, Ludwig, 207
Wizard of Oz, The, 3, 186

Yogachara tradition, 98, 124, 141
    eight consciousness in, 144–46
    and Madhyamaka, relationship between, 128–29, 137
    mistaken understandings of, 130–31
    names of, 137
    origins of, 128–29
    overview, 147–48
    See also three natures

zombie hypothesis, 73